EDITOR: Maryanne Blacker

FOOD EDITOR: Pamela Clark

■ ■ ■

ART DIRECTOR: Paula Wooller

DESIGNER: Robbylee Phelan

■ ■ ■

DEPUTY FOOD EDITOR: Jan Castorina

ASSISTANT FOOD EDITOR: Kathy Snowball

ASSOCIATE FOOD EDITOR: Enid Morrison

SENIOR HOME ECONOMISTS: Alexandra McCowan,
Louise Patniotis, Kathy Wharton

HOME ECONOMISTS: Cynthia Black, Leisel Chen,
Bronwen Clark, Kathy McGarry, Tracey Port,
Maggie Quickenden, Dimitra Stais

EDITORIAL COORDINATOR: Elizabeth Hooper

KITCHEN ASSISTANT: Amy Wong

■ ■ ■

STYLISTS: Wendy Berecry, Marie-Helene Clauzon,
Carolyn Fienberg, Jane Hann, Rosemary de Santis,
Christine Sheppard

PHOTOGRAPHERS: Kevin Brown, Robert Clark,
Robert Taylor, Jon Waddy

■ ■ ■

HOME LIBRARY STAFF

ASSISTANT EDITOR: Beverley Hudec

EDITORIAL COORDINATOR: Fiona Nicholas

■ ■ ■

PUBLISHER: Richard Walsh

DEPUTY PUBLISHER: Nick Chan

■ ■ ■

Produced by The Australian Women's Weekly Home Library.
Typeset by ACP Colour Graphics Pty Ltd. Colour
separations by Network Graphics Pty. Ltd. in Sydney. Printed
by Diamond Press Holdings Pty. Ltd. in Sydney.
Published by ACP Publishing Pty Ltd, 54 Park Street, Sydney.
♦ AUSTRALIA: Distributed by Network Distribution Company,
54 Park Street Sydney, (02) 282 8777.
♦ UNITED KINGDOM: Distributed in the U.K. by Australian
Consolidated Press (UK) Ltd, 20 Galowhill Rd, Brackmills,
Northampton NN4 OEE (0604) 760 456.
♦ CANADA: Distributed in Canada by Whitecap
Books Ltd, 1086 West 3rd St,
North Vancouver V7P 3J6 (604) 980 9852.
♦ NEW ZEALAND: Distributed in New Zealand by Netlink
Distribution Company, 17B Hargreaves St, Level 5,
College Hill, Auckland 1 (9) 302 7616.
♦ SOUTH AFRICA: Distributed in South Africa by Intermag,
PO Box 57394, Springfield 2137 (011) 493 3200.

■ ■ ■

Almost Vegetarian

Includes index.
ISBN 1 86396 015 5.

1. Cookery. 2. Entertaining. (Series:
Australian Women's Weekly Home
Library).

641.5'68

■ ■ ■

© A C P Publishing Pty Ltd 1993
ACN 053 273 546

■ ■ ■

COVER: Clockwise from left: Mushroom and Barley Cabbage
Rolls, page 54; Chilli Cheesy Pasta with Garlic Crumbs,
page 69; Baked Polenta with Two Cheeses, page 46.
*White china from Pillivuyt; patterned china from Villeroy & Boch;
glasses from Home & Garden on the Mall; background painted
with Porter's Boncote.*
OPPOSITE: Mexican Broad Bean Burgers, page 78.
BACK COVER: Spicy Chick Pea Naan with
Peach Chutney, page 91.

Almost Vegetarian

Outstanding and innovative recipes make this the best
vegetarian food you have ever tasted. But it is food for everyone,
because you can quickly add a little meat, seafood or poultry,
if you prefer. The delicious variety includes soups, snacks,
entrees, meals, accompaniments and salads for the family and
entertaining, all deftly surprising you with intriguing tastes and
textures. There are lovely dishes for all seasons, with
economical grains, pulses, vegetables, pastry and eggs enhanced
with lots of fresh herbs, spices, nuts, seeds and sauces.
The symbol ◎ indicates a variation, if desired.

Pamela Clark

FOOD EDITOR

BRITISH & NORTH AMERICAN READERS: Please note that
Australian cup and spoon measurements are metric. A quick conversion
guide appears on page 127.
A glossary explaining unfamiliar terms and ingredients appears on page 122.

Soups & Snacks

Lots of flavour surprises from around the world will delight you in this section.

The soups, for instance, include spicy corn chowder and tortilla crisps, while cauliflower,

ginger and barley soup is partnered by caraway seed damper. Even more inventive are

our snacks, an array of pleasures including fresh vegetables, waffles, pastries, crepes,

pancakes, vine leaf rolls, pizza, croquettes, easy dips and more. Some could double as

tempting entrees, such as beetroot timbales with butter sauce, tomato blinis

with eggplants and artichokes, egg and avocado sushi, or sun-dried tomato spring rolls

with garlic mayonnaise. They're all simple to put together.

The symbol ◉ indicates a variation, if desired.

BABY VEGETABLE APPETISERS

ARTICHOKES
375g jar artichoke hearts, drained, halved
1 tablespoon olive paste

TOMATOES
250g cherry tomatoes
½ cup (125ml) hummus
1 tablespoon chopped fresh parsley

SNOW PEAS
16 snow peas
125g packet cream cheese
1 teaspoon grated lemon rind
1 tablespoon lemon juice
50g soft butter
1 tablespoon chopped fresh dill

MUSHROOMS
16 button mushrooms
1 teaspoon olive oil
10g butter
1 teaspoon curry powder
¼ cup (40g) chopped macadamias

Artichokes: Top each artichoke half with ¼ teaspoon olive paste.
Tomatoes: Cut tops from tomatoes, scoop out seeds, drain tomatoes upside-down on absorbent paper for 30 minutes. Combine hummus and parsley in bowl, spoon mixture into piping bag fitted with plain tube, pipe mixture into tomatoes.
Snow Peas: Carefully split each pea along 1 side. Combine cheese, rind, juice, butter and dill in bowl, beat with electric mixer until smooth. Spoon mixture into piping bag fitted with star tube, pipe mixture into snow peas.
Mushrooms: Remove stems from mushrooms. Place mushrooms, stem side up, on oven tray, brush with oil, grill until mushrooms begin to soften; cool. Heat butter in pan, add curry powder and nuts, cook, stirring, until nuts are lightly browned; cool. Top mushrooms with curried nuts.
Serves 4.

- Recipe can be prepared several hours ahead.
- Storage: Covered, in refrigerator.
- Freeze: Not suitable.
- Microwave: Mushrooms suitable.

RIGHT: Baby Vegetable Appetisers.

BEETROOT TIMBALES WITH BUTTER SAUCE

1 bunch (about 500g) fresh beetroot, peeled, chopped
1 cup (250ml) water
¼ cup (60ml) white vinegar
1 tablespoon brown sugar
3 eggs, lightly beaten
2 tablespoons cream
⅓ cup (50g) plain flour
2 tablespoons chopped fresh chives

BUTTER SAUCE
¼ cup (20g) grated parmesan cheese
2 tablespoons cream
1 teaspoon cornflour
¼ cup (60ml) water
125g butter, chopped
2 tablespoons chopped fresh chives

Grease 6 timbale moulds (½ cup/125ml capacity). Combine beetroot, water, vinegar and sugar in pan, simmer, covered, until beetroot are tender; drain, cool.

Blend or process beetroot, eggs, cream and flour until smooth; stir in chives. Divide mixture between prepared moulds, place in baking dish; pour in enough boiling water to come halfway up sides of moulds. Bake, uncovered, in moderate oven about 40 minutes or until set. Stand 5 minutes, serve with butter sauce.
Butter Sauce: Combine cheese and cream with blended cornflour and 1 tablespoon of the water in pan, stir over heat until cheese melts. Whisk in butter, add remaining water and chives; reheat.
Serves 6.

■ Beetroot timbales can be made a day ahead.
■ Storage: Covered, in refrigerator.
■ Freeze: Not suitable.
■ Microwave: Beetroot suitable.

CHEESE WAFFLES WITH AVOCADO SALSA

¾ cup (110g) plain flour
¼ cup (35g) self-raising flour
1 teaspoon cumin seeds
1 teaspoon poppy seeds
2 teaspoons sugar
⅓ cup (40g) grated tasty cheese
⅓ cup (25g) grated parmesan cheese
1 egg, separated
¾ cup (180ml) milk
30g butter, melted
1 tablespoon water
¾ cup (180ml) sour cream

AVOCADO SALSA
2 limes
150g cherry tomatoes, halved
150g teardrop tomatoes, halved
½ medium red Spanish onion, sliced
1 small fresh red chilli, finely chopped
2 tablespoons chopped fresh coriander
1½ tablespoons lime juice
1 teaspoon sugar
1 medium avocado, chopped
1 cup loosely packed fresh purple basil leaves

Sift flours into bowl, stir in seeds, sugar and cheeses. Gradually stir in combined egg yolk, milk, butter and water. Beat egg white until soft peaks form, gently fold into mixture.

Drop ½ cup (125ml) mixture onto heated greased waffle iron. Close iron, cook about 2 minutes or until well browned. Repeat with remaining mixture. You will need 8 waffles for this recipe. Serve warm waffles with sour cream and avocado salsa.
Avocado Salsa: Using vegetable peeler, peel rind thinly from limes, cut rind into thin strips. Combine rind, tomatoes, onion, chilli and coriander in bowl, stir in combined juice and sugar, avocado and basil.
Serves 4.

■ Recipe best made just before serving.
■ Freeze: Waffles suitable.
■ Microwave: Not suitable.

◉ Add 1 cup (150g) chopped, smoked chicken to salsa.

ABOVE: Beetroot Timbales with Butter Sauce.
RIGHT: From back: Tomato and Mushroom Calzone, Cheese Waffles with Avocado Salsa.

Above: White under-plate from Villeroy & Boch.

TOMATO AND MUSHROOM CALZONE

2 teaspoons (7g) dried yeast
½ teaspoon sugar
½ cup (125ml) warm water
1 cup (150g) plain flour
½ cup (75g) cornmeal
½ teaspoon salt
2 tablespoons olive oil
1 tablespoon cornmeal, extra

TOMATO SAUCE
1 tablespoon olive oil
1 medium onion, finely chopped
2 cloves garlic, crushed
425g can tomatoes
¼ cup (60ml) tomato paste
1 teaspoon sugar
1 tablespoon chopped fresh oregano
2 teaspoons chopped fresh thyme

MUSHROOM FILLING
1 tablespoon olive oil
150g flat mushrooms, chopped
12 drained artichoke hearts, quartered
**2 tablespoons drained
    capers, chopped**
1 tablespoon chopped fresh dill

Lightly oil 30cm pizza pan. Combine yeast, sugar and water in bowl, stand about 10 minutes or until frothy. Combine flour, cornmeal and salt in bowl, stir in yeast mixture and oil, mix to a firm dough. Knead dough on floured surface about 8 minutes or until smooth and elastic.

Roll dough until large enough to fit prepared pan. Place dough on pan, spread with tomato sauce, leaving 3cm border. Spoon mushroom mixture over half the dough, brush border with water, fold over other half to enclose filling; fold edge to seal. Sprinkle with extra cornmeal. Stand calzone in warm place about 10 minutes or until risen. Bake in moderately hot oven about 35 minutes or until browned.

Tomato Sauce: Heat oil in pan, add onion and garlic, cook, stirring, until onion is soft. Add undrained crushed tomatoes and remaining ingredients, simmer, uncovered, about 15 minutes or until mixture is thickened slightly; cool.

Mushroom Filling: Heat oil in pan, add mushrooms, cook, stirring, until lightly browned and liquid is evaporated. Stir in artichokes, capers and dill.

Serves 4.

■ Tomato sauce and mushroom filling can be made a day ahead.
■ Storage: Covered, separately, in refrigerator.
■ Freeze: Tomato sauce suitable.
■ Microwave: Tomato sauce suitable.

◎ Add 60g chopped, smoked salmon to mushroom filling with artichokes.

GOATS' CHEESE AND RED PEPPER PARCELS

1 small red pepper
125g soft goats' cheese
8 pitted black olives, chopped
2 teaspoons chopped fresh thyme
4 sheets fillo pastry
100g butter, melted

Quarter pepper, remove seeds and membranes. Grill pepper, skin side up, until skin blisters and blackens. Peel away skin, chop pepper. Combine pepper, crumbled cheese, olives and thyme in bowl; mix well.

Layer 2 sheets of pastry together, brushing each with some of the butter. Cut pastry in half lengthways, cut each half into quarters. Place 2 level teaspoons of cheese mixture at 1 edge of each quarter, fold in edges, roll up to form parcels. Repeat with remaining pastry, butter and cheese mixture. Place on greased oven tray, brush with remaining butter. Bake in moderately hot oven about 15 minutes or until browned.

Makes 16.

■ Recipe best made close to serving.
■ Freeze: Uncooked parcels suitable.
■ Microwave: Not suitable.

◉ Add 60g chopped, smoked ham to goats' cheese mixture. Use 2 extra sheets of fillo pastry for this variation.

BUCKWHEAT CREPES WITH BLUE CHEESE AND BASIL

½ cup (75g) buckwheat flour
½ cup (75g) plain flour
2 eggs
1⅓ cups (330ml) milk
½ cup (60g) grated tasty cheese
½ teaspoon paprika

FILLING
60g butter
8 green shallots, chopped
½ cup (80g) pine nuts, toasted
200g blue cheese, crumbled
1 cup (125g) grated tasty cheese
2 tablespoons shredded fresh basil

Sift flours into bowl, gradually stir in combined eggs and milk, beat until smooth. Pour 2 to 3 tablespoons of batter into heated greased heavy-based pan, cook until browned underneath. Turn crepe, brown other side. Repeat with remaining mixture. You will need 12 crepes.

Divide filling evenly between crepes, roll up to enclose filling. Place crepes, seam side down, close together on greased oven trays. Top with cheese and paprika. Bake in moderately hot oven about 20 minutes or until browned and heated through.

Filling: Heat butter in pan, add shallots, cook, stirring, until soft. Combine shallot mixture with remaining ingredients in bowl; mix well.

Serves 4.

■ Recipe best made just before serving.
■ Freeze: Not suitable.
■ Microwave: Shallots suitable.

◉ Add 1 cup (200g) finely chopped, cooked chicken to filling.

SPICY CORN CHOWDER WITH TORTILLA CRISPS

6 corn cobs
2 tablespoons vegetable oil
2 medium onions, finely chopped
2 sticks celery, finely chopped
4 cloves garlic, crushed
2 teaspoons sambal oelek
1 tablespoon paprika
2 teaspoons cumin seeds
2 large potatoes, chopped
1 litre (4 cups) vegetable stock
300ml cream

TORTILLA CRISPS
3 packaged tortillas
oil for deep-frying

PEPPER AND PARSLEY PUREE
3 large red peppers
2 tablespoons chopped fresh parsley
½ cup (125ml) sour cream

Cut corn kernels from cobs. Heat oil in large pan, add onions, celery, garlic and spices, cook, stirring, until onions are soft. Stir in corn, potatoes and stock, simmer, covered, 1 hour. Add cream, stir until heated through. Top with pepper and parsley puree, serve with tortilla crisps.

Tortilla Crisps: Cut each tortilla into 12 triangles, deep-fry in batches in hot oil until lightly browned and crisp; drain on absorbent paper.

Pepper and Parsley Puree: Quarter peppers, remove seeds and membranes. Grill peppers, skin side up, until skin blisters and blackens; peel away skin. Blend or process peppers, parsley and cream until smooth.

Serves 6 to 8.

■ Recipe can be made a day ahead.
■ Storage: Chowder and puree, separately, covered, in refrigerator. Tortilla crisps, airtight container.
■ Freeze: Not suitable.
■ Microwave: Chowder suitable.

◉ Add 15 slices (150g) chopped, hot salami to finished chowder, stir until heated through.

LEFT: From back: Goats' Cheese and Red Pepper Parcels, Buckwheat Crepes with Blue Cheese and Basil.
ABOVE: Spicy Corn Chowder with Tortilla Crisps.

Left: China from Villeroy & Boch. Above: China from Country Road Homewear.

MUSHROOMS ON TOASTED RYE

60g butter
1 medium onion, chopped
1 clove garlic, crushed
200g large flat mushrooms, chopped
1 teaspoon seeded mustard
4 slices rye bread
4 slices tasty cheese
¼ cup (25g) drained sun-dried
    tomatoes, sliced

Heat half the butter in pan, add onion and garlic, cook, stirring, until onion is soft. Add remaining butter to pan, add mushrooms and mustard, cook, stirring, until mushrooms are soft.

Toast 1 side of bread, top other side with cheese, grill until cheese is melted. Place quarter of mushroom mixture on each slice, top with tomatoes.

Makes 4.

■ Recipe best made just before serving.
■ Freeze: Not suitable.
■ Microwave: Not suitable.

◉ Top tomatoes with 50g sliced pastrami, grill until heated through.

CORN AND RED PEPPER PINWHEELS

2 medium red peppers
2½ cups (375g) self-raising flour
½ cup (75g) plain flour
40g butter, chopped
⅓ cup (25g) grated parmesan cheese
1 tablespoon chopped fresh rosemary
3 teaspoons onion salt
½ cup (125ml) milk
⅔ cup (160ml) water, approximately
130g can creamed corn
2 tablespoons packaged
    breadcrumbs

Grease shallow 23cm round cake pan. Quarter peppers, remove seeds and membranes. Grill peppers, skin side up, until skin blisters and blackens. Peel away skin, chop peppers finely.

Sift flours into bowl, rub in butter. Stir in cheese, rosemary, salt, milk and enough water to form a soft dough.

Roll dough on floured surface into 24cm x 30cm rectangle. Starting at a long edge and leaving 4cm border along opposite edge, sprinkle peppers lengthways over half the dough. Cover centre half with combined corn and breadcrumbs.

Lightly brush border with water, tightly roll up rectangle from the red pepper side. Cut roll into 12 rounds. Place rounds, cut side down, in prepared pan. Bake pinwheels in moderately hot oven about 30 minutes or until browned. Serve pinwheels hot.

Makes 12.

■ Recipe can be prepared an hour ahead.
■ Freeze: Not suitable.
■ Microwave: Not suitable.

◉ Add 4 rashers chopped, cooked bacon. Sprinkle half the bacon over corn mixture on dough. Before baking, sprinkle remaining bacon over pinwheels.

CAULIFLOWER AND PEA SAMOSAS

1½ cups (225g) plain flour
30g butter
3 teaspoons poppy seeds
3 teaspoons sesame seeds
½ cup (125ml) warm water,
    approximately
oil for deep-frying

FILLING
1 tablespoon vegetable oil
½ small onion, finely chopped
1 teaspoon garam masala
1 teaspoon cumin seeds
1 teaspoon coriander seeds
pinch chilli powder
1 teaspoon paprika
100g cauliflower, finely chopped
⅔ cup (100g) frozen peas, thawed
¼ cup (60ml) coconut cream

Sift flour into bowl, rub in butter. Stir in seeds and enough water to form a firm dough. Knead dough on floured surface about 5 minutes or until smooth; cover, refrigerate 30 minutes.

Roll dough on lightly floured surface until 2mm thick. Cut into 8cm rounds. Spoon a level teaspoon of filling into centre of each round, lightly brush edges with water, fold over dough, using thumb and finger, fold over ends to seal. Deep-fry samosas in batches in hot oil until browned, drain on absorbent paper. Serve hot.

Filling: Heat oil in pan, add onion and spices, cook, stirring, until spices are fragrant. Add cauliflower, cook, stirring, until tender. Stir in peas and coconut cream; cool.

Makes about 30.

■ Uncooked samosas can be made a day ahead.
■ Storage: Covered, in refrigerator.
■ Freeze: Uncooked samosas suitable.
■ Microwave: Not suitable.

◉ Substitute 100g minced lamb for cauliflower in filling, cook, stirring, until mince is browned.

LEFT: Clockwise from back: Cauliflower and Pea Samosas, Corn and Red Pepper Pinwheels, Mushrooms on Toasted Rye.

China from Villeroy & Boch.

PITTA SALAD SANDWICH

150g button mushrooms, sliced
1 medium red Spanish onion, sliced
1 small green pepper, thinly sliced
¾ cup (120g) pitted black
   olives, chopped
100g feta cheese, crumbled
4 round pitta pocket breads
⅓ cup (80ml) hummus
1 small red coral lettuce

LEMON VINAIGRETTE
1 teaspoon grated lemon rind
2 tablespoons lemon juice
1 clove garlic, crushed
1 tablespoon chopped fresh mint
¼ cup (60ml) olive oil
1 teaspoon Dijon mustard

Combine mushrooms, onion, pepper, olives, cheese and vinaigrette in bowl; refrigerate 3 hours. Cut pocket breads in half. Spread hummus inside, fill with lettuce and mushroom mixture.

Lemon Vinaigrette: Combine all ingredients in jar; shake well.

Serves 4.

■ Mushroom mixture best prepared 3 hours ahead.
■ Storage: Covered, in refrigerator.
■ Freeze: Not suitable.

⊙ Add 3 slices (about 60g) chopped mortadella to mushroom mixture before refrigerating.

CHICK PEA CROQUETTES WITH HERB MAYONNAISE

1 tablespoon vegetable oil
1 medium onion, chopped
2 teaspoons tandoori curry mix
2 x 310g cans chick peas, drained
2 cloves garlic, crushed
2 teaspoons chopped fresh parsley
2 teaspoons chopped fresh coriander
plain flour
1 egg, lightly beaten
1 cup (70g) stale breadcrumbs
oil for deep-frying

HERB MAYONNAISE
2 egg yolks
1 clove garlic, crushed
1 teaspoon French mustard
1½ teaspoons white vinegar
½ cup (125ml) olive oil
1 tablespoon chopped fresh thyme
1 tablespoon chopped fresh parsley
1 tablespoon chopped fresh basil
1 tablespoon chopped
    fresh coriander

Heat oil in pan, add onion, cook, stirring, until soft, add curry mix, cook, stirring, until fragrant. Process chick peas, garlic and half the onion mixture until smooth, transfer to bowl, stir in remaining onion mixture and herbs.

Shape mixture into 16 croquettes. Roll croquettes in flour, shake away excess flour, dip into egg, then breadcrumbs. Deep-fry in batches in hot oil until golden brown; drain on absorbent paper. Serve with herb mayonnaise.

Herb Mayonnaise: Process yolks, garlic, mustard and vinegar until smooth. Gradually add oil in a thin stream while motor is operating, process until thick. Transfer mayonnaise to bowl, stir in herbs.

Makes 16.

- Uncooked croquettes and mayonnaise can be prepared a day ahead.
- Storage: Covered, separately, in refrigerator.
- Freeze: Not suitable.
- Microwave: Not suitable.

LAYERED VEGETABLE LOAF

1 ring-shaped loaf (about
    25cm diameter)
2 medium eggplants, thinly sliced
oil for shallow-frying
2 medium yellow peppers
2 medium red peppers
1 bunch (650g) English spinach
¼ cup (120g) pitted black
    olives, halved
200g smoked cheese, sliced

PESTO
1 cup firmly packed fresh basil leaves
2 tablespoons pine nuts, toasted
1 clove garlic, crushed
⅓ cup (80ml) olive oil

Split loaf in half, hollow out bread, leaving 2cm shell. Shallow-fry eggplants in batches in hot oil until lightly browned; drain on absorbent paper. Quarter peppers, remove seeds and membranes. Grill peppers, skin side up, until skin blisters and blackens. Peel away skin, cut peppers into thin strips. Boil, steam or microwave spinach until just wilted; drain, pat dry with absorbent paper.

Spread inside surfaces of bread with pesto, layer half with eggplant, peppers, spinach, olives and cheese, top with remaining bread.

Pesto: Blend or process all ingredients until smooth.

Serves 6 to 8.

- Recipe can be made a day ahead.
- Storage: Covered, in refrigerator.
- Freeze: Not suitable.
- Microwave: Spinach suitable.

◉ Layer 150g sliced, mild salami with remaining ingredients.

LEFT: From back: Chick Pea Croquettes with Herb Mayonnaise, Pitta Salad Sandwich. BELOW: Layered Vegetable Loaf.

Below: China and serviette from Country Road Homewear.

CHEESY SPINACH AND LEEK CREPE CAKE

¾ cup (110g) plain flour
3 eggs
15g butter, melted
1¼ cups (310ml) milk
½ cup (40g) grated parmesan cheese

SPINACH AND LEEK FILLING
40g butter
2 large leeks, sliced
4 cloves garlic, crushed
2 bunches (1.3kg) English spinach
1 teaspoon ground nutmeg
2 cups (160g) grated
    parmesan cheese
⅓ cup (50g) pine nuts, toasted

Grease 20cm springform tin. Sift flour into bowl, beat in combined eggs, butter and milk, beat until smooth. Cover, refrigerate 30 minutes.

Pour ¼ cup (60ml) of batter into heated greased heavy-based pan; cook until browned underneath. Turn crepe, brown other side. Repeat with remaining batter. You will need 8 crepes for this recipe.

Place 2 crepes into prepared tin, top with a third of the spinach and leek filling. Add 2 more crepes, then half the remaining filling, then 2 more crepes, then remaining filling and remaining crepes; sprinkle with cheese. Bake, uncovered, in moderate oven about 30 minutes or until heated through.

Spinach and Leek Filling: Heat butter in pan, add leeks and garlic, cook, stirring, until leeks are soft. Add spinach, cook, stirring, until wilted; drain. Combine spinach mixture and remaining ingredients in bowl, stir until combined.

Serves 4 to 6.

■ Crepes and filling can be made a day ahead.
■ Storage: Covered, separately, in refrigerator.
■ Freeze: Crepes suitable.
■ Microwave: Leeks and spinach suitable.

◉ Using 15 slices (180g) prosciutto, place 5 slices on each filling layer.

EGGPLANT MOUSSE WITH RATATOUILLE AND CROUTES

2 medium (about 660g) eggplants
30g butter
1 medium onion, finely chopped
2 cloves garlic, crushed
1 teaspoon ground cumin
⅔ cup (160ml) cream
90g butter, melted, extra
12 English spinach leaves

RATATOUILLE
1 medium zucchini
½ medium red pepper
½ medium green pepper
1 tablespoon olive oil
1 medium onion, finely chopped
1 clove garlic, crushed
2 medium tomatoes, peeled,
    seeded, chopped
2 tablespoons tomato paste
1 teaspoon chopped fresh thyme

CROUTES
1 small French bread stick
125g butter, melted

Cut eggplants in half lengthways, place, cut side down, on greased oven tray. Bake in moderate oven about 45 minutes or until eggplants are soft; cool.

Heat butter in pan, add onion, garlic and cumin, cook, stirring, until onion is soft. Scoop flesh from eggplants, discard skins. Blend or process eggplant and onion mixture until smooth. Transfer mixture to large bowl, stir in cream and extra butter, cover, refrigerate overnight.

Place 2 spinach leaves on each serving plate. Mould eggplant mixture into oval shapes using 2 wet tablespoons, place on spinach leaves. Serve mousse with ratatouille and croutes.

Ratatouille: Dice zucchini and peppers. Heat oil in pan, add onion and garlic, cook, stirring, until onion is soft. Stir in zucchini, peppers, tomatoes and paste. Simmer, uncovered, stirring occasionally, about 15 minutes or until vegetables are soft and mixture is thickened; cool, stir in thyme.

Croutes: Cut bread diagonally into thin slices, brush with butter. Place on oven trays, bake in moderate oven about 15 minutes or until golden brown and crisp.

Serves 6.

■ Recipe can be made 2 days ahead.
■ Storage: Mousse and ratatouille, in refrigerator. Croutes, airtight container.
■ Freeze: Not suitable.
■ Microwave: Ratatouille suitable.

RIGHT: From left: Cheesy Spinach and Leek Crepe Cake, Eggplant Mousse with Ratatouille and Croutes.

Plates from Primex Products; serviette from Piper Bishop Aust Pty Ltd.

PARATHAS WITH FRESH MINT CHUTNEY

2 cups (300g) plain flour
2 teaspoons garam masala
1 tablespoon vegetable oil
⅔ cup (160ml) water, approximately
100g ghee, approximately

FILLING
30g ghee
1 medium onion, finely chopped
2 cloves garlic, crushed
1 tablespoon grated fresh ginger
1 tablespoon curry powder
1 teaspoon ground cumin
1½ cups (120g) shredded
    Chinese cabbage
1 medium carrot, grated
½ cup (40g) bean sprouts
30g snow pea sprouts, chopped
2½ tablespoons coconut milk

FRESH MINT CHUTNEY
1 cup firmly packed fresh mint leaves
2 green shallots, chopped
1 clove garlic, crushed
¼ teaspoon sambal oelek
2 tablespoons lemon juice
1 teaspoon garam masala
1 teaspoon sugar
2 tablespoons water
2 tablespoons toasted coconut

Sift flour and garam masala into bowl, stir in oil and enough water to mix to a soft dough. Turn dough onto lightly floured surface, knead about 5 minutes or until smooth. Cover dough, stand 1 hour.

Divide dough into 8 pieces, roll each piece to a 22cm round. Divide filling into 8 portions, place 1 portion on a circle, spread to 9cm.

Fold in each side so that filling is completely covered, sealing over-lapping pastry with a little water, to form a 10cm square parcel.

Roll parcel gently with rolling pin to seal and flatten. Repeat with remaining dough and filling. Heat half the ghee in large heavy-based pan, add parathas in batches, cook until puffed and browned on both sides; drain on absorbent paper. Use remaining ghee, if necessary. Serve warm with fresh mint chutney.

Filling: Heat ghee in pan, add onion, garlic and ginger, cook, stirring, until onion is soft. Add curry powder and cumin, cook, stirring, until fragrant. Stir in remaining ingredients, cook, stirring, until vegetables are cooked.

Fresh Mint Chutney: Process mint, shallots, garlic, sambal oelek, juice, garam masala, sugar and water until smooth; stir in coconut.

Makes 8.

■ Recipe can be prepared a day ahead.
■ Storage: Covered, in refrigerator.
■ Freeze: Not suitable.
■ Microwave: Not suitable.

◉ Add 1 cup (160g) chopped, cooked lamb to filling.

MINTY COUSCOUS IN VINE LEAVES

½ cup (125ml) vegetable stock
½ cup (100g) couscous
4 green shallots, chopped
1 tablespoon roasted unsalted
    peanuts, chopped
1 tablespoon chopped fresh mint
3 teaspoons lemon juice
2 teaspoons light soy sauce
2 tablespoons chopped raisins
200g vine leaves in brine,
    rinsed, drained
1 cup (250ml) water
1 tablespoon tomato paste
2 teaspoons hoi sin sauce

Bring stock to boil in pan, remove from heat, stir in couscous, stand about 5 minutes or until stock is absorbed. Stir in shallots, peanuts, mint, lemon juice, soy sauce and raisins.

Place 2 vine leaves over-lapping on bench, spoon 1 level tablespoon couscous mixture in centre of vine leaves, fold in sides, roll up to enclose filling. Repeat with remaining vine leaves and couscous mixture. Line base of heavy-based pan

with any remaining vine leaves. Place rolls in single layer in pan, pour in combined water, paste and sauce. Place upturned plate on top of rolls to prevent rolls moving during cooking, cover with tight-fitting lid, simmer 12 minutes. Serve warm or cold.

Makes about 15.

■ Recipe can be made 2 days ahead.
■ Storage: Covered, in refrigerator.
■ Freeze: Not suitable.
■ Microwave: Not suitable.

SUN-DRIED TOMATO SPRING ROLLS

50g rice vermicelli noodles
½ cup (65g) drained chopped
    sun-dried tomatoes
1 tablespoon chopped fresh chives
2 teaspoons chopped fresh oregano
1 clove garlic, crushed
2 tablespoons grated
    parmesan cheese
20 spring roll wrappers
1 egg, lightly beaten
oil for deep-frying

GARLIC MAYONNAISE
2 cloves garlic, crushed
1 egg
⅔ cup (160ml) extra light olive oil

Cover noodles with boiling water, stand 10 minutes. Drain noodles on absorbent paper. Chop noodles finely.

Combine noodles, tomatoes, herbs, garlic and cheese in bowl. Brush edge of wrappers with egg, place 1 level tablespoon of tomato mixture in a corner of each wrapper. Roll up wrappers diagonally, folding in edges to enclose filling. Deep-fry spring rolls in batches in hot oil until lightly browned; drain on absorbent paper. Serve with garlic mayonnaise.

Garlic Mayonnaise: Blend or process garlic and egg until smooth. Add oil gradually in a thin stream while motor is operating; process until thick.

Makes 20.

■ Mayonnaise can be made a
    day ahead.
■ Storage: Covered, in refrigerator.
■ Freeze: Spring rolls suitable.
■ Microwave: Not suitable.

◉ Add ½ cup (100g) finely chopped, cooked chicken to sun-dried tomato mixture. You will need 6 extra spring roll wrappers.

LEFT: Clockwise from left: Minty Couscous in Vine Leaves, Parathas with Fresh Mint Chutney, Sun-Dried Tomato Spring Rolls.

Plate and bowls from Accoutrement; basket from Country Road Homewear.

ASPARAGUS, POACHED EGGS WITH SORREL HOLLANDAISE

20g butter
½ cup (35g) stale breadcrumbs
1 tablespoon chopped fresh parsley
2 bunches (about 500g) fresh asparagus spears
4 eggs, poached

SORREL HOLLANDAISE
2 egg yolks
2 teaspoons white wine vinegar
200g butter, melted
1 tablespoon warm water
1 tablespoon chopped fresh sorrel

Heat butter in pan, add crumbs, cook, stirring, until browned, stir in parsley. Boil, steam or microwave asparagus until tender. Divide asparagus between 4 plates, top with eggs, pour over hollandaise, sprinkle with crumb mixture.

Sorrel Hollandaise: Combine egg yolks and vinegar in heatproof bowl, whisk over pan of simmering water until thick. Remove from heat, gradually whisk in butter, stir in water and sorrel.

Serves 4.

■ Recipe best made just before serving.
■ Freeze: Not suitable.
■ Microwave: Asparagus suitable.

◉ Serve with 160g sliced, smoked salmon.

BOCCONCINI AND TOMATO KEBABS

1 small French bread stick
30g butter, melted
32 (300g) baby bocconcini
32 (250g) cherry tomatoes
2 tablespoons pine nuts, toasted

CORIANDER DRESSING
2 tablespoons chopped fresh coriander roots and stems
1 cup firmly packed fresh coriander leaves
2 cloves garlic, crushed
2 tablespoons pine nuts, toasted
2 tablespoons grated parmesan cheese
¼ cup loosely packed fresh basil leaves
¼ teaspoon sambal oelek
½ cup (125ml) olive oil

Cut 20 x 1cm slices of bread, cut slices in half. Brush slices with butter, place on oven tray in single layer, bake in moderate oven about 10 minutes or until crisp.

Thread bread, bocconcini and tomatoes onto 8 skewers, beginning and ending with bread slice. Place kebabs on oven tray, bake in moderate oven about 5 minutes or until cheese begins to soften. Serve kebabs topped with coriander dressing, sprinkle with nuts.

Coriander Dressing: Process coriander roots, stems and leaves, garlic, nuts, cheese, basil, sambal oelek and half the oil until smooth. Gradually add remaining oil in a thin stream while motor is operating, process until smooth.

Serves 4.

■ Coriander dressing can be made a day ahead.
■ Storage: Covered, in refrigerator.
■ Freeze: Not suitable.
■ Microwave: Not suitable.

◉ Cut 8 drained anchovy fillets into quarters, thread onto skewers between tomatoes and bocconcini.

POTATO PANCAKES

2 tablespoons vegetable oil
1 small red Spanish onion,
 finely chopped
4 medium (about 600g) old potatoes
⅓ cup (50g) sesame seeds, toasted
1 tablespoon cornflour
⅔ cup (160ml) vegetable oil, extra

SAUCE
1 teaspoon cornflour
2 tablespoons water
⅓ cup (80ml) salt-reduced soy sauce
¼ cup (60ml) rice vinegar
2 teaspoons sesame oil

Heat oil in pan, add onion, cook, stirring, until soft, remove from heat; cool. Coarsely grate potatoes. Combine onion mixture, potatoes, seeds and cornflour in bowl.

Heat 2 tablespoons of the extra oil in heavy-based frying pan. Spread ¼ cup (60ml) potato mixture into pan (cook 3 at a time), cook on both sides until well browned and crisp; drain on absorbent paper. Repeat with remaining extra oil and mixture. Serve pancakes topped with sauce.
Sauce: Blend cornflour and water in small pan, stir in remaining ingredients, stir over heat until mixture boils and thickens.

Serves 4.

■ Pancakes best made just before serving.
■ Freeze: Not suitable.
■ Microwave: Sauce suitable.

◉ Heat 30g butter in pan, add 4 lightly beaten eggs and ⅔ cup (160ml) milk. Stir gently over low heat until eggs are still creamy and slightly firm. Serve scrambled eggs on potato pancakes, top with sauce.

LEFT: Asparagus, Poached Eggs with Sorrel Hollandaise.
BELOW: From left: Potato Pancakes, Bocconcini and Tomato Kebabs.

Below: China from Villeroy & Boch.

CAULIFLOWER, GINGER AND BARLEY SOUP

½ cup (100g) pearl barley
1 tablespoon vegetable oil
1 medium onion, finely chopped
2 cloves garlic, crushed
1 tablespoon grated fresh ginger
½ teaspoon turmeric
1 teaspoon coriander
**   seeds, crushed**
1 teaspoon cumin seeds
1 medium apple, peeled, grated
1 medium carrot, chopped
1.75 litres (7 cups) vegetable stock
1 small cauliflower, chopped
¼ cup chopped fresh coriander

Place barley in bowl, cover well with boiling water, stand 1 hour; drain.

Heat oil in large pan, add onion and garlic, cook, stirring, until onion is soft. Add ginger, turmeric and seeds, cook, stirring, until fragrant. Add barley, apple and carrot, cook, stirring, 2 minutes, add stock, simmer, covered, 1 hour. Add cauliflower, cook, covered, further 10 minutes or until cauliflower is tender; stir in coriander. Serve with caraway seed damper.

Serves 6 to 8.

■ Recipe can be made a day ahead.
■ Storage: Covered, in refrigerator.
■ Freeze: Not suitable.
■ Microwave: Suitable.

◉ Add 1 cup (150g) chopped, cooked chicken to soup with coriander, stir until heated through.

CARAWAY SEED DAMPER

2 cups (300g) white self-raising flour
1 cup (160g) wholemeal
**   self-raising flour**
125g soft butter
2 teaspoons caraway seeds
2 tablespoons sunflower seed kernels
1 tablespoon sesame seeds
½ cup (125ml) milk
¼ cup (60ml) water, approximately

Sift flours into bowl, rub in butter, stir in seeds. Stir in milk and enough water to mix to a soft dough. Knead dough on floured surface until smooth. Press dough into 16cm round, place on greased oven tray. Cut a cross about 1cm deep in dough, brush with a little extra milk. Bake in moderately hot oven about 30 minutes or until damper is well browned and sounds hollow when tapped.

■ Recipe best made just before serving.
■ Freeze: Suitable.
■ Microwave: Not suitable.

GAZPACHO

8 medium tomatoes, peeled, quartered
1 large green cucumber,
**   peeled, seeded, chopped**
1 medium green pepper, chopped
1 small onion, chopped
2 cloves garlic, crushed
1 cup (70g) stale breadcrumbs
2 cups (500ml) vegetable stock
⅓ cup (80ml) olive oil
¼ cup (60ml) white wine vinegar
1 small green cucumber,chopped, extra

Blend or process tomatoes, cucumber, pepper, onion, garlic, crumbs and stock in batches until combined. Transfer to large bowl; stir in oil and vinegar. Cover, refrigerate until cold. Serve sprinkled with extra cucumber.

Serves 6.

■ Recipe can be made several hours ahead.
■ Storage: Covered, in refrigerator.
■ Freeze: Not suitable.

◉ Heat 1 cup (250ml) water and 1 cup (250ml) dry white wine in large pan, add 2kg small mussels, cook, covered, until shells open; drain. Remove mussels from shells, discard shells. Add cold mussels to gazpacho with extra cucumber.

LEFT: Clockwise from left: Cauliflower, Ginger and Barley Soup, Caraway Seed Damper, Gazpacho.
ABOVE: Tomato Lentil Soup with Curried Croutons.

Left: China from Home & Garden on the Mall; basket from Country Road Homewear.
Above: China from Country Road Homewear; tiles from Country Floors.

TOMATO LENTIL SOUP WITH CURRIED CROUTONS

30g butter
1 clove garlic, crushed
2 medium onions, chopped
1 large carrot, finely chopped
⅓ cup (70g) brown lentils
425g can tomatoes
3 cups (750ml) vegetable stock
1 cup (250ml) water

CURRIED CROUTONS
4 slices white bread
2 tablespoons vegetable oil
2 teaspoons curry powder

Heat butter in pan, add garlic, onions and carrot, cook, stirring, until onions are soft. Add lentils, undrained crushed tomatoes, stock and water. Simmer, covered, stirring occasionally, about 20 minutes or until lentils are tender. Serve with curried croutons.
Curried Croutons: Remove crusts from bread, cut each slice into 8 triangles, brush with combined oil and curry powder. Place triangles on oven tray in single layer, bake, uncovered, in moderately hot oven about 10 minutes or until crisp.

Serves 4.

■ Recipe can be made a day ahead.
■ Storage: Soup, covered, in refrigerator. Croutons, airtight container.
■ Freeze: Not suitable.
■ Microwave: Soup suitable.

◉ Add 3 slices (about 30g) chopped prosciutto to carrot mixture in pan.

EGG AND AVOCADO SUSHI

2 cups (440g) nishiki rice
2 cups (500ml) water
1 piece konbu seaweed
½ teaspoon sugar
½ teaspoon salt
¼ cup (60ml) mirin
¼ cup (60ml) rice vinegar
2 eggs, lightly beaten
1 small green cucumber
4 sheets nori seaweed
½ teaspoon wasabi paste
¼ cup (75g) pickled pink
  ginger, drained
½ medium avocado, sliced

Combine rice, water and konbu in heavy-based saucepan, bring to boil, cover with tight-fitting lid, simmer over low heat 20 minutes. Remove from heat, do not remove lid, stand 10 minutes.

Transfer rice to bowl, discard konbu. Combine sugar, salt, mirin and vinegar in small pan, stir until sugar is dissolved, stir into hot rice; cool.

Pour eggs into heated greased pan, cook until set; cool, cut into long strips. Cut cucumber into long strips.

Place 1 sheet of nori seaweed on bench, spread quarter of the rice over two-thirds of seaweed. Spread rice with a little wasabi. Place quarter of egg, cucumber, ginger and avocado in a row 5cm from 1 edge of rice. Roll seaweed around filling to form a log, wetting seaweed edges to seal. Wrap in plastic wrap, refrigerate until firm. Repeat with remaining seaweed,

rice, wasabi, egg, cucumber, ginger and avocado. Slice rolls, serve with extra light soy sauce and extra pickled pink ginger, if desired.

Makes about 24.

■ Recipe can be made several hours ahead.
■ Storage: Covered, in refrigerator.
■ Freeze: Not suitable.
■ Microwave: Not suitable.

 Add 100g smoked salmon to filling, using a quarter for each roll.

TOMATO BLINIS WITH EGGPLANTS AND ARTICHOKES

2 teaspoons (7g) dried yeast
½ teaspoon sugar
⅔ cup (160ml) warm milk
1 egg, separated
1 egg yolk
½ cup (125ml) sour cream
1 cup (150g) plain flour
½ teaspoon salt
12 cherry tomatoes, halved

EGGPLANTS AND ARTICHOKES
2 tablespoons olive oil
2 cloves garlic, crushed
3 baby eggplants, sliced
3 medium zucchini, sliced
⅓ cup (80ml) balsamic vinegar
12 drained artichoke hearts, halved
½ cup (90g) small black olives
⅓ cup shredded fresh basil

Combine yeast, sugar and half the milk in small bowl, cover, stand in warm place about 10 minutes or until mixture is frothy. Stir in combined egg yolks, sour cream and remaining milk.

Sift flour and salt into large bowl. Gradually stir in yeast mixture, stir until mixture is smooth; cover, stand in warm place about 45 minutes or until batter rises and is slightly bubbly.

Beat egg white in small bowl until firm peaks form, fold into batter, cover, stand in warm place about 45 minutes or until mixture is bubbly.

Place 4 tomato halves, cut side down, about 6cm apart on heated greased heavy-based pan. Spoon 1 tablespoon of batter onto each tomato half, cook until lightly browned underneath. Turn blinis, brown other side. Repeat with remaining tomato halves and batter. Serve with eggplants and artichokes.

Eggplants and Artichokes: Heat oil in pan, add garlic, eggplants and zucchini, cook, stirring, 4 minutes. Add vinegar, artichokes and olives, cook, stirring occasionally, until eggplants are tender; stir in basil.

Serves 6 to 8.

■ Recipe best made just before serving.
■ Freeze: Not suitable.
■ Microwave: Not suitable.

 Add 500g scallops to pan with vinegar, artichokes and olives, cook, stirring, until heated through.

BRIOCHE SANDWICHES WITH CREAMY TOMATO FILLING

1 large brioche
1 egg, lightly beaten
1 tablespoon sesame seeds
⅔ cup (160ml) sour cream
½ stick celery, finely chopped
2 tablespoons slivered
    almonds, toasted
1 tablespoon seeded mustard
1 tablespoon chopped fresh chives
2 medium tomatoes, sliced
6 lettuce leaves

Cut brioche into 16 slices, brush 1 side of each slice with a little egg, sprinkle with seeds. Place slices, seed side down, in heated greased pan, cook until lightly browned underneath. Turn slices, brown other side; drain on absorbent paper.

Combine cream, celery, nuts, mustard and chives in bowl; mix well. Place 8 brioche slices, seed side down, on bench, spread with cream mixture, top with tomato, lettuce and remaining brioche.

Makes 8.

■ Recipe best made close to serving.
■ Freeze: Not suitable.
■ Microwave: Not suitable.

◉ Add 2 rashers chopped, cooked bacon to sour cream mixture.

LEFT: Egg and Avocado Sushi.
ABOVE: From back: Tomato Blinis with Eggplants and Artichokes, Brioche Sandwiches with Creamy Tomato Filling.

Left: Australian ceramics from Mura Clay Gallery.
Above: Box from Home & Garden on the Mall; tiles from Country Floors.

21

FOUR DIPS WITH CRUDITES AND FRENCH BREAD

2 medium carrots
2 sticks celery
200g snow peas
1 small French bread stick, sliced

PARSLEY AND PEPPER DIP
2 large red peppers
1 cup firmly packed chopped fresh
**   flat-leafed parsley**
2 cloves garlic, crushed
2 tablespoons lemon juice
⅓ cup (80ml) olive oil
1 tablespoon pine nuts, toasted

TOMATO CAPER TAPENADE
¾ cup (80g) drained sun-dried
**   tomatoes, chopped**
¼ cup (60ml) olive oil
¼ cup (45g) drained capers
2 cloves garlic, crushed
1 teaspoon grated lemon rind
1 tablespoon lemon juice
1 teaspoon chopped fresh thyme

TOFU PATE
½ cup (80g) sunflower seed kernels
150g tofu, chopped
1 tablespoon olive oil
2½ tablespoons wheatgerm
½ medium carrot, grated
1 teaspoon chopped fresh dill

MUSHROOM GARLIC DIP
60g butter
500g button mushrooms, sliced
2 cloves garlic, crushed
1 small onion, chopped
1 cup (250ml) sour cream
2 tablespoons chopped
**   fresh coriander**

Cut carrots and celery into 6cm sticks. Serve carrot, celery, snow peas and bread with dips.

Parsley and Pepper Dip: Quarter peppers, remove seeds and membranes. Grill peppers, skin side up, until skin blisters and blackens. Peel away skin, chop peppers finely. Combine peppers, parsley, garlic, juice and oil in bowl; top with nuts.

Makes about 1½ cups (375ml).

Tomato Caper Tapenade: Process all ingredients until finely minced. Top with extra capers, if desired.

Makes about 1 cup (250ml).

Tofu Pate: Process half the seeds until finely ground. Add tofu, oil and wheatgerm; process until combined. Stir in remaining seeds, carrot and dill.

Makes about 1 cup (250ml).

Mushroom Garlic Dip: Heat butter in pan, add mushrooms, garlic and onion, cook, stirring, until liquid is evaporated. Process mushroom mixture until finely minced, combine in bowl with cream and coriander; mix well. Cover, refrigerate until cold.

Makes about 2½ cups (625ml)

■ Dips can be prepared a day ahead.
■ Storage: Covered, in refrigerator.
■ Freeze: Not suitable.
■ Microwave: Not suitable.

NEW POTATO AND GRILLED PEPPER PIZZA

2 large red peppers
¼ cup (60ml) olive oil
2 medium red Spanish onions, sliced
2 cloves garlic, crushed
1 tablespoon chopped fresh oregano
250g baby new potatoes, sliced
2 cups (200g) grated
**   mozzarella cheese**
½ cup (80g) pitted black
**   olives, halved**

PIZZA DOUGH
15g compressed yeast
1 teaspoon sugar
¼ cup (60ml) warm water
1½ cups (225g) plain flour
½ teaspoon salt
¼ cup (60ml) warm milk
1 tablespoon olive oil

Grease 30cm pizza pan. Quarter peppers, remove seeds and membranes. Grill peppers, skin side up, until skin blisters and blackens. Peel away skin, cut peppers into thin strips.

Heat 1 tablespoon of the oil in pan, add onions and garlic, cook, stirring, until onions are soft, stir in oregano. Remove onion mixture from pan. Heat remaining oil in same pan, add potatoes in batches, cook until lightly browned on both sides; drain on absorbent paper.

Roll pizza dough on floured surface until large enough to fit prepared pan. Spread onion mixture over dough, top with half the cheese, potatoes, olives, pepper and remaining cheese. Bake in moderately hot oven about 30 minutes or until browned and cooked through.

Pizza Dough: Combine yeast and sugar in small bowl, stir in water, cover, stand in warm place about 10 minutes or until mixture is frothy.

Sift flour and salt into large bowl, stir in yeast mixture, milk and oil, mix to a firm dough. Turn dough onto floured surface, knead about 5 minutes or until dough is smooth and elastic. Place dough in oiled bowl, cover, stand in warm place about 30 minutes or until doubled in size.

Serves 2 to 4 .

■ Recipe best made just before serving.
■ Freeze: Suitable.
■ Microwave: Not suitable.

◉ Add 200g chopped pancetta or ham to cooked onion mixture.

LEFT: Four Dips with Crudites and French Bread. Clockwise from top: Tofu Pate, Parsley and Pepper Dip, Mushroom Garlic Dip, Tomato Caper Tapenade.
BELOW: New Potato and Grilled Pepper Pizza.

Left: China and tray from Home & Garden on the Mall. Below: China from Country Road Homewear.

Pastry & Eggs

With eggs and pastry, you have the basis of limitless recipes for the family or entertaining. As a light meal or entree, consider our fresh corn and pea souffles, leek and yellow pepper flan, curried pumpkin and sesame tartlets, or pepper and sweet onion pastries. Much more homely are hot, hearty pies: one has potatoes layered with onion, herbs and cream in a double pastry case. Eggs, of course, are great in sauces, fillings and pastry, or star in their own right in an onion, cabbage and sage frittata, and a herb omelette with beetroot potato cakes. We suggest different types of pastry to make, and others to buy for speed and convenience. The symbol ◉ indicates a variation, if desired.

●

LEEK AND YELLOW PEPPER FLAN

1¼ cups (180g) plain flour
100g cold butter, chopped
1 egg yolk
1 tablespoon water, approximately
1 yellow pepper
60g butter, extra
1 tablespoon olive oil
1 medium onion, sliced
2 medium leeks, sliced
1 tablespoon chopped fresh dill
2 eggs
½ cup (125ml) cream
¼ cup (20g) grated parmesan cheese

Grease 11cm x 35cm rectangular or 24cm round flan tin. Sift flour into bowl, rub in butter. Stir in egg yolk and enough water to make ingredients cling together. Press dough into a ball, knead on floured surface until smooth, cover, refrigerate 30 minutes.

Roll dough on floured surface until large enough to line prepared tin, ease pastry into tin, trim edges. Place tin on oven tray, line pastry with baking paper, fill with dried beans or rice. Bake in moderately hot oven 10 minutes, remove paper and beans, bake further 10 minutes or until browned; cool.

Halve pepper, remove seeds and membranes. Grill pepper, skin side up, until skin blisters and blackens. Peel away skin, cut pepper into thin strips. Heat extra butter and oil in pan, add onion and leeks, cook, stirring, until leeks are soft; drain on absorbent paper.

Spread pepper strips over pastry base, top with leek mixture, sprinkle with dill. Pour combined eggs and cream over leek mixture, sprinkle with cheese. Bake in moderate oven about 35 minutes or until set and browned.

Serves 4.

■ Recipe can be made a day ahead.
■ Storage: Covered, in refrigerator.
■ Freeze: Suitable.
■ Microwave: Not suitable.

◉ Substitute 100g flaked, smoked trout for yellow pepper.

RIGHT: Leek and Yellow Pepper Flan.
China from Villeroy & Boch.

FRESH CORN AND PEA SOUFFLES

⅓ cup (35g) packaged breadcrumbs
3 fresh corn cobs
125g butter, chopped
⅓ cup chopped fresh chives
¼ cup chopped fresh chervil
2 tablespoons chopped fresh thyme
⅓ cup (50g) plain flour
2 cups (500ml) milk
¾ cup (60g) grated parmesan cheese
1 cup (125g) frozen peas, thawed
6 eggs, separated

Grease 6 souffle dishes (1¼ cup/310ml capacity), sprinkle with breadcrumbs, shake away excess breadcrumbs.

Cut corn kernels from cobs. Heat butter in pan, add corn and herbs, cook, stirring occasionally, over low heat 10 minutes. Add flour, cook, stirring, until mixture is bubbly. Remove from heat, gradually stir in milk, stir over heat until mixture boils and thickens. Stir in cheese and peas.

Transfer corn mixture to large bowl, stir in egg yolks. Beat egg whites in medium bowl with electric mixer until soft peaks form. Fold egg whites into corn mixture in 2 batches. Pour evenly into prepared dishes, place dishes on oven tray. Bake in moderately hot oven about 20 minutes or until well risen and browned.

Makes 6.

■ Recipe must be made just before serving.
■ Freeze: Not suitable.
■ Microwave: Not suitable.

◉ Add 4 rashers chopped, cooked bacon to mixture with egg yolks.

ABOVE: *From left: Pepper and Sweet Onion Pastries with Pesto, Fresh Corn and Pea Souffles.*

Plate from Primex Products.

PEPPER AND SWEET ONION PASTRIES WITH PESTO

2 sheets ready-rolled puff pastry
1 egg yolk
40g butter
2 medium red Spanish onions, sliced
2 tablespoons water
⅓ cup (65g) brown sugar
½ cup (125ml) brown vinegar
2 large red peppers
2 large yellow peppers
8 fresh asparagus spears, halved

PESTO
1½ cups firmly packed fresh
     basil leaves
⅓ cup (80ml) olive oil
2 cloves garlic, crushed
¼ cup (25g) drained sun-dried
     tomatoes, chopped
½ cup (40g) grated romano cheese
1 tablespoon balsamic vinegar
2 teaspoons water

Make base pattern by cutting 12.5cm square from paper. Make frame pattern by cutting another 12.5cm square from paper; inside this, cut an 8.5cm square, leaving 2cm frame.

Using base pattern, cut 4 squares from 1 sheet of pastry. Place squares onto greased oven trays.

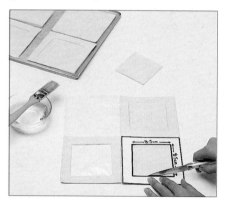

Using frame pattern, cut 4 frame shapes from 1 sheet of pastry; discard scraps. Brush edges of bases with water, press frames onto bases, forming shallow pastry cases. Cover, refrigerate several hours or overnight.

Brush tops of frames with egg yolk, prick bases with fork, bake in very hot oven about 6 minutes or until pastry is browned and risen; cool.

Heat butter in pan, add onions and water, cook, covered, over low heat about 15 minutes, stirring occasionally, or until onions are soft. Add sugar and vinegar, simmer, uncovered, further 15 minutes or until thick; drain, discard liquid.

Quarter peppers, remove seeds and membranes. Grill peppers, skin side up, until skin blisters and blackens. Peel away skins, cut peppers into thin strips; cool.

Boil, steam or microwave asparagus until just tender; drain, rinse under cold water, drain. Divide onion mixture, peppers and asparagus between pastry cases; top with pesto.

Pesto: Blend or process all ingredients until well combined.

Serves 4.

- Pastry cases can be made a day ahead.
- Storage: Airtight container.
- Microwave: Asparagus suitable.
- Freeze: Not suitable.

◉ Divide 4 canned, drained, chopped anchovies between pastry cases.

ONION, CABBAGE AND SAGE FRITTATA

¼ cup (60ml) olive oil
3 medium onions, sliced
2 cloves garlic, crushed
¼ small (about 250g)
    cabbage, shredded
⅓ cup (80ml) dry white wine
2 teaspoons sugar
¼ cup chopped fresh sage
8 eggs, lightly beaten
½ cup (125ml) cream
¾ cup (60g) grated parmesan cheese
2 tablespoons olive oil, extra

TOMATO SAUCE
2 tablespoons olive oil
1 medium onion, sliced
2 cloves garlic, thinly sliced
¼ teaspoon sambal oelek
2 x 425g cans tomatoes
½ teaspoon sugar
¼ cup chopped fresh thyme

Heat oil in pan, add onions and garlic, cook, covered, stirring occasionally, about 30 minutes or until onions are very soft. Stir in cabbage, wine, sugar and sage, cook, stirring, until wine is evaporated; drain on absorbent paper, cool.

Combine eggs, cream, cheese and onion mixture in bowl; mix well. Heat extra oil in 27cm ovenproof pan, pour in egg mixture, cook over very low heat about 10 minutes or until mixture is starting to set. Place pan in moderately slow oven, cook further 15 minutes or until set. Serve with tomato sauce.

Tomato Sauce: Heat oil in pan, add onion, garlic and sambal oelek, cook, stirring, until onion is soft. Stir in undrained crushed tomatoes, sugar and thyme, simmer, uncovered, about 15 minutes or until sauce is thickened.

Serves 4 to 6.

- Tomato sauce can be made a day ahead.
- Storage: Covered, in refrigerator.
- Freeze: Not suitable.
- Microwave: Not suitable.

 Add 185g can drained, flaked tuna to tomato sauce, stir until hot.

HERB OMELETTE WITH BEETROOT POTATO CAKES

1 medium onion, grated
2 small (about 200g) fresh
   beetroot, grated
250g white sweet potato, grated
⅔ cup (100g) plain flour
1 egg
2 teaspoons sweet chilli sauce
⅓ cup (25g) grated parmesan cheese
2 tablespoons vegetable oil

HERB OMELETTE
4 eggs
1 tablespoon chopped
   fresh coriander
1 tablespoon chopped fresh chives

DRESSING
⅔ cup (160ml) vegetable oil
2 tablespoons white vinegar
2 teaspoons sugar
½ teaspoon sesame oil
1 tablespoon hoi sin sauce
½ teaspoon sambal oelek

Combine onion, beetroot, potato, flour, egg, sauce and cheese in bowl. Divide mixture into 4 portions. Heat oil in pan, drop each portion into pan, flatten into a round shape about 1½cm thick. Cook potato cakes until browned underneath, turn, brown other side; drain on absorbent paper. Serve topped with herb omelette strips; drizzle with dressing.

Herb Omelette: Beat 1 egg with 1 teaspoon of the coriander and 1 teaspoon of the chives in bowl. Pour mixture into heated greased pan, cook until lightly browned underneath and set; remove from pan. Repeat with remaining eggs and herbs. Cut omelettes into strips.

Dressing: Combine all ingredients in jar; shake well.

Serves 4.

■ Dressing can be made a day ahead.
■ Storage: Covered, in refrigerator.
■ Freeze: Not suitable.
■ Microwave: Not suitable.

◉ Top beetroot potato cakes with omelette strips and 150g thinly sliced roast beef.

LEFT: From left: Onion, Cabbage and Sage Frittata, Herb Omelette with Beetroot Potato Cakes.

POTATO AND HERB PIE

3 medium potatoes
50g butter
1/4 cup (60ml) olive oil
1 medium onion, sliced
2 tablespoons chopped fresh parsley
2 teaspoons chopped fresh thyme
1/2 cup (125ml) milk
1/2 cup (125ml) cream
1 egg, lightly beaten
1 egg, lightly beaten, extra
1 sheet ready-rolled puff pastry

PASTRY
1 cup (150g) plain flour
90g cold butter
1 egg yolk
1 tablespoon lemon juice,
    approximately

Cut potatoes into 5mm slices. Heat butter
and oil in pan, add potatoes in batches,
cook until lightly browned and tender;
drain on absorbent paper, cool.

Add onion to same pan, cook, stirring,
until onion is soft; drain on absorbent
paper, cool.

Layer potatoes, onion and herbs in
pastry case, pour over combined milk,
cream and egg. Brush edge of pastry
case with a little extra egg, top pie with puff
pastry, trim edges; gently press edges to
seal. Brush pastry with remaining extra
egg, prick pastry with fork.

Bake in moderately hot oven 15
minutes, reduce heat to moderate, bake
further 40 minutes or until pastry is puffed
and browned. Stand pie 10 minutes
before serving.

Pastry: Sift flour into bowl, rub in butter.
Add egg yolk and enough juice to mix to a
firm dough. Press ingredients together to
form a ball, cover, refrigerate 30 minutes.

Roll pastry between baking paper until
large enough to line 25cm pie dish. Ease
pastry into side of dish, trim edge, cover,
refrigerate 20 minutes.

Line pastry case with paper, fill with
dried beans or rice. Bake in moderately
hot oven 10 minutes, remove paper and
beans, bake further 10 minutes or until
browned; cool.

Serves 6.

■ Recipe can be made a day ahead.
■ Storage: Covered, in refrigerator.
■ Freeze: Not suitable.
■ Microwave: Not suitable.

◉ Add 180g finely chopped speck to
pan with onion.

PUMPKIN AND SESAME TARTLETS

*You will need about 400g peeled,
seeded pumpkin for this recipe.*

1 3/4 cups (260g) plain flour
1 1/2 teaspoons ground cumin
125g cold butter, chopped
2 tablespoons sesame seeds
1 egg yolk
1 tablespoon water, approximately
1 tablespoon sunflower seed kernels
2 teaspoons cumin seeds
2 teaspoons sesame seeds, extra

FILLING
1 cup (250ml) cold cooked
    mashed pumpkin
1/2 cup (125ml) cream
2 eggs, lightly beaten
1 clove garlic, crushed
2 teaspoons curry powder
1/2 teaspoon garam masala
2 tablespoons chopped
    fresh coriander
2 green shallots, chopped

Grease 6 x 10cm flan tins. Sift flour and
cumin into bowl, rub in butter. Stir in
sesame seeds, egg yolk and enough
water to make ingredients cling together.
Knead dough gently on floured surface
until smooth, cover, refrigerate 30 minutes.

Divide dough into 6 portions, roll each
portion to fit prepared tin. Ease pastry into
tins, trim edges, place tins on oven tray,
cover, refrigerate 30 minutes.

Line pastry cases with paper, fill with
dried beans or rice, place on oven tray.
Bake in moderately hot oven 10 minutes,
remove paper and beans, bake further 10
minutes or until browned; cool.

Pour filling into pastry cases, bake in
moderate oven 10 minutes, sprinkle with
combined remaining seeds. Bake further
20 minutes or until filling is set.

Filling: Combine all ingredients in bowl;
mix well.

Makes 6.

■ Recipe best made on day of serving.
■ Storage: Covered, in refrigerator.
■ Freeze: Not suitable.
■ Microwave: Pumpkin suitable.

◉ Add 3 rashers chopped, cooked
bacon to filling.

*LEFT: From left: Pumpkin and Sesame
Tartlets, Potato and Herb Pie.*

*Plates from Primex Products; rug from Piper Bishop
Aust. Pty Ltd; fork from Jarass Pty Ltd.*

SUN-DRIED TOMATO AND ZUCCHINI QUICHE

½ cup (100g) cottage cheese
100g soft butter
1⅓ cups (200g) plain flour
1 tablespoon olive oil
1 medium onion, sliced
¼ cup (35g) drained chopped
    sun-dried tomatoes
⅓ cup (70g) drained
    sun-dried zucchini
¼ cup shredded fresh basil
¾ cup (60g) grated gruyere cheese
¼ cup (20g) grated parmesan cheese
3 eggs
¾ cup (180ml) cream
¼ cup (30g) grated tasty cheese

Combine cottage cheese and butter in bowl, stir in flour. Press dough into a ball, knead gently on floured surface until smooth, cover, refrigerate 30 minutes.

Roll dough on floured surface until large enough to line 24cm flan tin, ease pastry into tin, trim edge. Place tin on oven tray, line pastry with paper, fill with dried beans or rice. Bake in moderately hot oven 10 minutes, remove paper and beans, bake further 10 minutes or until browned.

Heat oil in pan, add onion, cook until soft; drain on absorbent paper. Spread onion, tomatoes, zucchini, basil, gruyere and parmesan into pastry case, pour over combined eggs and cream, sprinkle with tasty cheese. Bake in moderate oven about 35 minutes or until set.

Serves 6.

■ Recipe can be made a day ahead.
■ Storage: Covered, in refrigerator.
■ Freeze: Not suitable.
■ Microwave: Not suitable.

◉ Add 3 chopped, cooked bacon rashers to filling.

RIGHT: Cheesy Vegetable Pie.
BELOW: From left: Red Pepper and Artichoke Strudel, Sun-Dried Tomato and Zucchini Quiche.

Right: Plate from Primex Products; cutlery from Jarass Pty Ltd; placemat from Piper Bishop Aust. Pty Ltd. Below: Plate from Accoutrement.

RED PEPPER AND ARTICHOKE STRUDEL

3 large red peppers
20 artichoke hearts, drained, halved
1/3 cup shredded fresh basil
1/3 cup (50g) pine nuts, toasted
1 cup (200g) cottage cheese
1 tablespoon Dijon mustard
8 sheets fillo pastry
50g butter, melted
1 tablespoon Dijon mustard, extra

Quarter peppers, remove seeds and membranes. Grill peppers, skin side up, until skin blisters and blackens. Peel away skin, cut peppers into 3cm pieces. Combine peppers, artichokes, basil, nuts, cheese and mustard in bowl; mix well.

Layer pastry sheets, brushing each with some of the combined butter and extra mustard. Spoon filling along 1 long side of pastry, leaving 4cm border. Fold in sides, roll up firmly to enclose filling; brush with remaining butter mixture. Place strudel on greased oven tray. Bake in moderately hot oven about 25 minutes or until browned and heated through.

Serves 4.

- Recipe can be prepared a day ahead.
- Storage: Covered, in refrigerator.
- Freeze: Not suitable.
- Microwave: Not suitable.

○ Use only 2 peppers and 10 artichoke hearts for filling; add 1kg cooked, shelled prawns to filling.

CHEESY VEGETABLE PIE

2 cups (300g) white plain flour
1 cup (160g) wholemeal plain flour
250g packet cream cheese, chopped
125g cold butter, chopped
2 eggs
1 egg yolk
1 tablespoon water, approximately
1 cup (125g) grated tasty cheese
1 tablespoon sesame seeds

VEGETABLE FILLING
60g butter
1/4 cup (40g) plain flour
2 cups (500ml) milk
2 tablespoons seeded mustard
2/3 cup (80g) grated tasty cheese
300g turnip
125g parsnip
1 medium carrot
1 medium onion
1 medium potato
175g kumara
200g cauliflower
1 cup (125g) frozen peas, thawed

Sift flours into bowl, rub in cheese and butter. Stir in 1 of the eggs, egg yolk and enough water to make ingredients cling together. Press dough into a ball, knead gently on floured surface until smooth, cover, refrigerate 30 minutes.

Roll half the dough on floured surface until large enough to fit 30cm pizza pan. Top with vegetable filling, leaving 1cm border; sprinkle filling with two-thirds of the cheese. Brush border with some of the remaining egg.

Roll out remaining dough, place over vegetable mixture, press edges to seal; trim. Mark edges with fork. Brush top with remaining egg, sprinkle with remaining cheese and seeds. Bake in moderate oven about 45 minutes or until browned.

Vegetable Filling: Melt butter in pan, add flour, stir over heat until bubbling. Remove from heat, gradually stir in milk, stir over heat until mixture boils and thickens. Remove from heat, stir in mustard and cheese; cool.

Cut turnip, parsnip, carrot, onion, potato, kumara and cauliflower into 2cm pieces. Boil, steam or microwave all vegetables, except peas, until just tender; drain, rinse under cold water, drain. Combine vegetables and peas in large bowl, stir in cheese sauce; mix well.

- Vegetable filling can be made a day ahead.
- Storage: Covered, in refrigerator.
- Freeze: Not suitable.
- Microwave: Vegetables suitable.

○ Add 250g sliced, smoked turkey or chicken to vegetable filling.

Grains

Start exploring the fabulous range of grains with us, and see how readily they blend with other ingredients in a great variety of enticing dishes. Grains are also very filling, an economical way to serve a lot of people. In our glossary, we picture the grains we have used; with their earthy colours and different shapes they are fascinating little packages of high nutrition, with protein, fibre and complex carbohydrates. Barley, burghul, millet, cornmeal and couscous are all here, plus several types of rice. However, if you can't obtain the rice we specify, simply use brown or white rice, although the flavour will be slightly different.

The symbol ◉ *indicates a variation, if desired.*

CRUNCHY RICE SQUARES WITH AVOCADO SALAD

2 sticks celery, thinly sliced
1 medium avocado, chopped
1 small red pepper, thinly sliced
½ cup (75g) unsalted
    roasted peanuts

RICE SQUARES
¼ cup (45g) wild rice
1 cup (200g) short-grain rice
2 cups (500ml) water
1 vegetable stock cube
1 tablespoon chopped
    fresh coriander
oil for deep-frying

DRESSING
1½ tablespoons light soy sauce
1½ teaspoons sugar
½ cup (125ml) vegetable oil
¼ cup (60ml) white vinegar
1½ teaspoons sesame oil
1 small fresh red chilli, finely chopped

Combine celery, avocado, pepper, peanuts, rice squares and half the dressing in bowl; mix lightly to combine, drizzle with remaining dressing.

Rice Squares: Grease 15cm square cake pan, line base and sides with foil, grease foil. Add wild rice to pan of boiling water, boil, uncovered, about 35 minutes or until tender; drain. Combine short-grain rice, water and crumbled stock cube in pan, bring to boil, simmer, covered, about 12 minutes or until all liquid is absorbed and rice is sticky. Stir in wild rice and coriander.

Press mixture firmly into prepared pan, smooth top. Cover with greased foil, top with a piece of plastic-covered cardboard, weigh down with cans. Refrigerate several hours or overnight.

Remove rice mixture from pan, cut into 2cm squares. Deep-fry rice squares in batches in hot oil until browned and crisp; drain on absorbent paper.

Dressing: Combine all ingredients in jar; shake well.

Serves 4.

- Rice squares and dressing can be prepared a day ahead.
- Storage: Covered, separately, in refrigerator.
- Freeze: Not suitable.
- Microwave: Rices suitable.

◉ Add 750g cooked, shelled prawns to salad just before serving.

RIGHT: Crunchy Rice Squares with Avocado Salad.

China from Noritake.

SPICY FRUIT 'N' NUT BARLEY SALAD

2 cups (400g) pearl barley
¼ cup (60ml) vegetable oil
1 large onion, finely chopped
1 tablespoon grated lemon rind
2 teaspoons grated fresh ginger
2 teaspoons cardamom seeds
2 tablespoons turmeric
2 teaspoons ground cumin
½ cup (75g) shelled
  pistachios, toasted
¼ cup (40g) roasted buckwheat
¼ cup (35g) sesame seeds, toasted
¼ cup (40g) pepitas
¾ cup (120g) chopped pitted dates
¾ cup (140g) chopped dried figs
4 dried pear halves, chopped
2 sticks celery, finely chopped
½ cup (125ml) lemon juice
¾ cup (180ml) mayonnaise

Add barley to large pan of boiling water, boil, uncovered, about 40 minutes or until tender; drain.

Heat oil in pan, add onion, rind, ginger and spices, cook, stirring, until onion is soft. Combine barley, onion mixture and remaining ingredients in bowl; mix well.

Serves 6 to 8.

■ Recipe can be made a day ahead.
■ Storage: Covered, in refrigerator.
■ Freeze: Not suitable.
■ Microwave: Barley suitable.

◉ Add 2 cups (about 300g) shredded, cooked beef to salad.

RED PEPPERS WITH VEGETABLE COUSCOUS

6 large red peppers
1 cup (180g) couscous
1 cup (250ml) boiling water
20g butter, melted
¼ cup (35g) dried currants
2 tablespoons vegetable oil
1 medium onion, finely chopped
1 clove garlic, crushed
1 teaspoon ground coriander
2 teaspoons ground cumin
1 tablespoon grated fresh ginger
1 medium carrot, chopped
1 medium eggplant, chopped
1 medium potato, chopped
1 cup (80g) shredded cabbage
1 medium tomato, chopped
1 cup (250ml) vegetable stock
450g can chick peas, drained

Cut off stem end of peppers 2cm from top; reserve ends. Carefully remove seeds and membranes from peppers.

Place couscous in heatproof bowl, add water, stand 5 minutes. Add butter and currants; stir gently with fork.

Heat half the oil in pan, add onion, garlic, coriander, cumin and ginger, cook, stirring, until fragrant. Add remaining vegetables, tomato, stock and chick peas, simmer, uncovered, stirring occasionally, about 20 minutes or until vegetables are tender; stir in couscous mixture. Fill peppers with couscous mixture. Place peppers in ovenproof dish, replace stem ends; brush with remaining oil. Bake, uncovered, in moderate oven about 45 minutes or until peppers are tender.

Serves 6.

■ Recipe can be prepared
  3 hours ahead.
■ Storage: Covered, in refrigerator.
■ Freeze: Not suitable.
■ Microwave: Suitable.

◉ Replace cabbage with 150g cooked, minced lamb. Add to couscous mixture before filling peppers.

RIGHT: From left: Spicy Fruit 'n' Nut Barley Salad, Red Peppers with Vegetable Couscous.

China from Noritake.

BAKED OMELETTE WITH OAT BRAN TOPPING

30g butter
2 medium zucchini, thinly sliced
2 green shallots, chopped
150g mushrooms, chopped
2 teaspoons chopped fresh thyme
6 eggs
¾ cup (180ml) cream

OAT BRAN TOPPING
½ cup (60g) oat bran
2 tablespoons grated parmesan
  cheese
2 tablespoons grated gruyere cheese
1 medium tomato, seeded, chopped

Heat butter in pan, add zucchini, shallots and mushrooms, cook, stirring, until vegetables are soft; add thyme. Beat eggs and cream in bowl until combined.

Spread vegetable mixture over base of ovenproof dish (1 litre/4 cup capacity). Pour over egg mixture, top with oat bran topping, place in baking dish with enough boiling water to come halfway up side of dish. Bake, uncovered, in moderate oven about 45 minutes or until set.

Oat Bran Topping: Combine all ingredients in bowl; mix well.

Serves 4.

- ▓ Recipe best made close to serving.
- ▓ Freeze: Not suitable.
- ▓ Microwave: Not suitable.

◉ Add 1½ cups (225g) chopped, cooked chicken to vegetable mixture before placing in ovenproof dish.

NUTTY RICE WITH FIGS AND APRICOTS

1 teaspoon cumin seeds
2 tablespoons sunflower seed kernels
2 tablespoons pepitas
1 cup (200g) white rice
1 cup (200g) brown rice
½ cup (75g) dried apricots, sliced
½ cup (95g) dried figs, chopped
1 cup (150g) unsalted
  roasted cashews
⅓ cup (50g) pine nuts, toasted
⅔ cup (110g) almond kernels

DRESSING
¼ cup (60ml) red wine vinegar
½ cup (125ml) olive oil
2 teaspoons chopped fresh oregano
2 teaspoons chopped fresh chives

Add seeds and pepitas to dry pan, stir over heat until cumin seeds begin to pop. Add rices to separate pans of boiling water, boil, uncovered, until tender; drain, cool.

Combine seed mixture, rices and remaining ingredients in bowl, add dressing; mix well.

Dressing: Combine all ingredients in jar; shake well.

Serves 4.

- ▓ Recipe can be made 3 hours ahead.
- ▓ Storage: Covered, in refrigerator.
- ▓ Freeze: Not suitable.
- ▓ Microwave: Rices suitable.

◉ Grill 2 white fish cutlets; cool, flake into pieces. Top salad with fish.

RICE AND LENTIL BURGERS WITH MUSTARD CREAM

1 cup (200g) red lentils
½ cup (100g) white rice
½ cup (100g) brown rice
½ cup (60g) packaged
  ground almonds
1 medium onion, grated
1 vegetable stock cube
½ cup (125ml) sour cream
1 tablespoon seeded mustard
2 teaspoons chopped fresh thyme
1 cup (70g) stale breadcrumbs
1 cup (100g) packaged breadcrumbs
oil for shallow-frying
6 hamburger buns, split, toasted
50g snow pea sprouts
1 large avocado, sliced

MUSTARD CREAM
⅓ cup (80ml) sour cream
⅓ cup (80ml) mayonnaise
1 tablespoon Dijon mustard
2 teaspoons seeded mustard
1 tablespoon chopped fresh chives

Add lentils to pan of boiling water, simmer, uncovered, about 5 minutes or until lentils are tender; drain (do not rinse). Add rices to separate pans of boiling water, simmer, uncovered, until tender; drain (do not rinse).

Process lentils, rices and nuts until combined, refrigerate until cold. Combine lentil mixture, onion, crumbled stock cube, cream, mustard, thyme and stale breadcrumbs in bowl; mix well.

Divide mixture into 6 patties, toss patties in packaged breadcrumbs, press crumbs on firmly, cover, refrigerate 1 hour. Shallow-fry patties in hot oil until lightly browned on both sides and heated through. Place patties on base of buns, top with sprouts, avocado and mustard cream; replace tops.

Mustard Cream: Combine all ingredients in bowl, mix well; refrigerate until cold.

Serves 6.

- ▓ Patties and mustard cream can be made a day ahead.
- ▓ Storage: Covered, separately, in refrigerator.
- ▓ Freeze: Patties suitable.
- ▓ Microwave: Lentils and rices suitable.

◉ Place a slice of ham on base of each bun before topping with patties.

FAR LEFT: From left: Nutty Rice with Figs and Apricots, Baked Omelette with Oat Bran Topping.
LEFT: Rice and Lentil Burgers with Mustard Cream.

Far left: China from Villeroy & Boch. Left: China from The Bay Tree.

VEGETABLE RICE CAKE WITH MUSTARD CHEESE SAUCE

1 cup (200g) short-grain rice
5 medium (about 500g) zucchini
650g kumara

MUSTARD CHEESE SAUCE
60g butter
1 medium onion, finely chopped
2 cloves garlic, crushed
½ cup (75g) plain flour
¼ cup (60ml) dry white wine
2 cups (500ml) milk
¼ cup (60ml) sour cream
¼ cup (20g) grated parmesan cheese
¼ cup (30g) grated gruyere cheese
1 tablespoon chopped
**   fresh rosemary**
2 tablespoons seeded mustard

TOPPING
¾ cup (50g) stale breadcrumbs
15g butter, melted
1 tablespoon chopped fresh thyme
¼ cup (20g) grated parmesan cheese

Grease 23cm springform tin, line base with paper, grease paper. Add rice to large pan of boiling water, boil, uncovered, until tender; drain, rinse under cold water, drain well.

Cut zucchini and kumara into 7mm slices. Boil, steam or microwave zucchini and kumara separately until just tender. Rinse zucchini under cold water; drain.

Combine rice and 1½ cups (375ml) of the mustard cheese sauce in bowl. Spread half the rice mixture over base of prepared pan, press down firmly. Place half the zucchini on rice mixture, spread with some of remaining sauce. Top with half the kumara slices, spread with more of the sauce. Repeat with remaining zucchini, kumara, sauce and rice mixture. Sprinkle with topping, place on oven tray. Bake in moderate oven about 40 minutes or until topping is browned.

Mustard Cheese Sauce: Heat butter in pan, add onion and garlic, cook, stirring, until onion is soft. Add flour, stir until dry and grainy. Remove pan from heat, gradually stir in combined wine and milk, stir over heat until mixture boils and thickens. Stir in cream, cheeses, rosemary and mustard.

Topping: Combine all ingredients in bowl; mix well.

Serves 6.

- Recipe can be made a day ahead.
- Storage: Covered, in refrigerator.
- Freeze: Not suitable.
- Microwave: Rice, zucchini and kumara suitable.

◉ Sprinkle 4 chopped, cooked bacon rashers between layers.

40

MILLET AND TOFU PATTIES WITH HORSERADISH CREAM

1 teaspoon sesame oil
1 tablespoon vegetable oil
1 medium onion, finely chopped
1 stick celery, finely chopped
2 teaspoons grated fresh ginger
1 teaspoon paprika
¼ cup (50g) red lentils
⅓ cup (80ml) water
1 tablespoon light soy sauce
375g packet tofu, drained
1 tablespoon packaged breadcrumbs
1 egg, lightly beaten
1 tablespoon milk
⅔ cup (50g) millet flakes
¼ cup (40g) pepitas
oil for shallow-frying

HORSERADISH CREAM
⅓ cup (80ml) sour cream
2 tablespoons vegetable oil
1 tablespoon seeded mustard
1 tablespoon horseradish cream
¼ cup (50g) soft cream cheese
1 teaspoon grated fresh ginger

Heat oils in pan, add onion, celery, ginger and paprika, cook, stirring, until onion is soft. Add lentils, stir until combined. Add water, simmer, uncovered, stirring occasionally, until all liquid is evaporated. Transfer mixture to large bowl.

Process soy sauce and tofu until smooth. Combine lentil mixture, tofu mixture and breadcrumbs in bowl; mix well. Cover, refrigerate 3 hours.

Divide mixture into 8 patties. Dip patties in combined egg and milk, toss in combined millet and pepitas. Shallow-fry patties in hot oil until lightly browned on both sides; drain on absorbent paper. Serve with horseradish cream.
Horseradish Cream: Combine all ingredients in bowl.

Makes 8.

- Uncooked patties and horseradish cream can be prepared a day ahead.
- Storage: Covered, separately, in refrigerator.
- Freeze: Not suitable.
- Microwave: Not suitable.

◉ Replace lentils with 100g minced chicken; add to pan with onion.

BAKED TOMATOES WITH FRAGRANT RICE

6 large firm tomatoes
1 tablespoon vegetable oil
1 teaspoon grated fresh ginger
¼ cup (60ml) vegetable oil, extra
6 cloves
2 cardamom pods
⅓ cup (45g) slivered almonds
1 cup (200g) basmati rice
2 cups (500ml) water
1 cinnamon stick
30g butter
2 cloves garlic, crushed
1 cup (125g) frozen peas, thawed
2 tablespoons chopped fresh parsley

Cut tops from tomatoes; reserve tops. Scoop out pulp, seeds and juice; strain. You will need 1 cup (250ml) juice. Discard pulp and seeds.

Heat oil in pan, add ginger, cook, stirring, 1 minute, add reserved juice, boil, uncovered, until reduced by half.

Heat extra oil in pan, add cloves, cardamom and nuts, cook, stirring, until nuts are lightly browned. Stir in rice, then water and cinnamon, bring to boil, cook, covered tightly, over low heat about 15 minutes or until rice is tender and liquid absorbed.

Remove from heat, stand, covered, 5 minutes; discard whole spices and cinnamon stick. Stir in butter, garlic, peas, half the tomato mixture and parsley.

Divide mixture between tomatoes, spoon over remaining tomato mixture; replace tops. Place tomatoes in baking dish with enough boiling water to come 1cm up sides of tomatoes. Brush tops with a little oil. Bake, uncovered, in moderately slow oven about 45 minutes or until tomatoes are just tender.

Serves 6.

- Recipe best made just before serving.
- Freeze: Not suitable.
- Microwave: Not suitable.

◉ Substitute 125g cooked, minced lamb for peas.

ABOVE LEFT: At back and right: Vegetable Rice Cake with Mustard Cheese Sauce; in front: Millet and Tofu Patties with Horseradish Cream.
RIGHT: Baked Tomatoes with Fragrant Rice.

Above left: Patterned plates are Johnson Brothers china from Waterford Wedgwood Australia Ltd.
Right: Oval dish from Primex Products; fork from Jarass Pty Ltd.

TOMATO BEAN CASSEROLES WITH BURGHUL TOPPING

¾ cup (150g) dried kidney beans
¾ cup (150g) dried chick peas
2½ cups (375g) frozen broad beans
2 tablespoons vegetable oil
3 cloves garlic, sliced
1 medium leek, chopped
2 sticks celery, chopped
1 medium carrot, chopped
2 x 425g cans tomatoes
¼ cup (60ml) tomato paste
2 teaspoons cumin seeds

BURGHUL TOPPING
1 cup (160g) burghul
½ cup (75g) sesame seeds, toasted
1 cup (80g) grated parmesan cheese

Place kidney beans and chick peas in separate bowls, cover well with water, cover, stand overnight.

Drain kidney beans and chick peas, place in separate pans, cover with water, simmer, covered, until tender; drain. Add broad beans to pan of boiling water, simmer, uncovered, 1 minute, drain; cool. Remove skins from broad beans.

Heat oil in pan, add garlic, leek, celery and carrot, cook, stirring, until leek is soft. Add undrained crushed tomatoes, paste, seeds, kidney beans, chick peas and broad beans, simmer, uncovered, about 10 minutes or until thickened slightly.

Spoon mixture evenly into 6 ovenproof dishes (1 cup/250ml capacity). Sprinkle with burghul topping. Bake, uncovered, in moderate oven about 20 minutes or until heated through and browned.

Burghul Topping: Place burghul in heatproof bowl, cover with boiling water, stand 15 minutes; drain, rinse under cold water, drain. Blot dry with absorbent paper. Combine burghul, seeds and cheese in bowl; mix well.

Serves 6.

- ■ Recipe can be made a day ahead.
- ■ Storage: Covered, in refrigerator.
- ■ Freeze: Suitable.
- ■ Microwave: Not suitable.

◉ Use only ½ cup (100g) kidney beans and ½ cup (100g) chick peas in this recipe. Add 4 cooked, sliced, thick sausages to tomato mixture before placing in ovenproof dishes.

CREAMY BARLEY WITH TOMATOES AND MUSHROOMS

2 cups (400g) pearl barley
60g butter
2 cloves garlic, crushed
1 medium onion, sliced
250g button mushrooms, sliced
410g can tomatoes, drained, chopped
⅓ cup (55g) chopped pitted
    black olives
1 tablespoon chopped fresh chives
1 tablespoon chopped fresh basil
1 cup (250ml) sour cream
½ cup (40g) grated parmesan cheese
1 cup (125g) grated tasty cheese
2 fresh medium tomatoes, sliced
¼ cup (15g) stale breadcrumbs

Grease deep ovenproof dish (2 litre/8 cup capacity). Add barley to large pan of boiling water, boil, uncovered, about 40 minutes or until tender; drain.

Heat butter in pan, add garlic, onion and mushrooms, cook, stirring, until onion is soft and liquid evaporated. Combine barley, mushroom mixture, canned tomatoes, olives, herbs, cream, parmesan cheese and half the tasty cheese in bowl; mix well.

Spoon barley mixture into prepared dish. Place fresh tomato slices around edge of dish. Sprinkle casserole with combined remaining cheese and breadcrumbs. Bake, uncovered, in moderately hot oven about 40 minutes or until browned.

Serves 6.

- ■ Recipe can be made 3 hours ahead.
- ■ Storage: Covered, in refrigerator.
- ■ Freeze: Not suitable.
- ■ Microwave: Barley suitable.

◉ Add 250g sliced, cooked lamb fillets to barley mixture.

COUSCOUS, ORANGE AND SPINACH SALAD

2 cups (500ml) vegetable stock
2 cups (360g) couscous
80g butter
1 bunch (about 650g) English spinach
1 medium red pepper
¾ cup (120g) chopped pitted dates
3 medium oranges, segmented
3 green shallots, chopped
1 cup (150g) unsalted
    roasted cashews

ORANGE DRESSING
2 tablespoons white wine vinegar
2 teaspoons balsamic vinegar
1 teaspoon grated orange rind
⅓ cup (80ml) orange juice
½ teaspoon sugar

Add stock to pan, bring to boil, stir in couscous; remove from heat, stand 3 minutes. Add butter, stir over heat until butter is melted; cool.

Boil, steam or microwave spinach until just wilted; rinse under cold water, drain on absorbent paper.

Quarter pepper, remove seeds and membranes. Grill pepper, skin side up, until skin blisters and blackens. Peel away skin, chop pepper.

Combine couscous, spinach, pepper and remaining ingredients in bowl, add orange dressing; mix well.

Orange Dressing: Combine all ingredients in jar; shake well.

Serves 6.

- ■ Recipe can be made 3 hours ahead.
- ■ Storage: Covered, in refrigerator.
- ■ Freeze: Not suitable.
- ■ Microwave: Spinach suitable.

◉ Serve salad with grilled or barbecued chicken.

LEFT: Clockwise from left: Creamy Barley with Tomatoes and Mushrooms, Couscous, Orange and Spinach Salad, Tomato Bean Casseroles with Burghul Topping.

SAFFRON COUSCOUS WITH RAISINS AND ALMONDS

½ cup (100g) chick peas
1½ cups (270g) couscous
1 cup (250ml) hot vegetable stock
½ cup (125ml) hot water
2 tablespoons olive oil
4 small onions, quartered
2 cloves garlic, sliced
¼ teaspoon ground saffron
½ teaspoon garam masala
1 teaspoon paprika
½ cup (85g) raisins
1 medium yellow zucchini,
   thinly sliced
1 medium carrot, thinly sliced
¼ cup (60ml) sherry vinegar
⅓ cup (55g) almond kernels,
   roasted, chopped

Place chick peas in bowl, cover well with water, cover, stand overnight.

Drain chick peas, add to pan of boiling water, boil, uncovered, about 30 minutes or until tender; drain.

Place couscous in large bowl, pour over combined stock and water, cover, stand until liquid is absorbed. Add 1 tablespoon of the oil, mix lightly with fork.

Heat remaining oil in pan, add onions, cook, stirring, until browned. Add garlic and spices, cook, stirring, until fragrant. Stir in raisins, zucchini and carrot, cook, stirring, about 3 minutes or until vegetables are just tender; stir in vinegar. Combine chick peas, couscous, vegetable mixture and nuts in bowl.

Serves 4.

- ■ Recipe can be made 3 hours ahead.
- ■ Storage: Covered, in refrigerator.
- ■ Freeze: Not suitable.
- ■ Microwave: Not suitable.

◉ Add 4 cooked, sliced lamb fillets to bowl before serving.

TOMATO RICE SLICE

1¼ cups (250g) white long-grain rice
1 bunch (about 650g) English spinach
1 tablespoon vegetable oil
1 small red Spanish onion, chopped
2 tablespoons chopped fresh dill
⅓ cup (40g) grated gruyere cheese
¾ cup (90g) grated tasty cheese
3 eggs, lightly beaten
¾ cup (180ml) cream
2 medium tomatoes, sliced
1 cup (125g) grated tasty
   cheese, extra

Grease 23cm square slab cake pan. Add rice to pan of boiling water, boil, uncovered, until tender; drain. Boil, steam or microwave spinach until just wilted; rinse under cold water, drain well.

Heat oil in pan, add onion, cook, stirring, until soft. Combine rice, spinach, onion, dill and both cheeses in bowl, stir in combined eggs and cream; mix well.

44

Spread mixture evenly into prepared pan, place tomato slices over rice mixture, sprinkle with extra cheese. Bake, uncovered, in moderate oven about 35 minutes or until set and lightly browned.

Serves 4 to 6.

- ■ Recipe best made close to serving.
- ■ Freeze: Not suitable.
- ■ Microwave: Rice and spinach suitable.

◉ Add 440g can drained, flaked salmon to rice mixture.

RICE WITH CURRANTS AND RED PEPPERS

1¼ cups (250g) long-grain rice
2 medium red peppers
1 medium red Spanish onion,
   finely chopped
½ cup (75g) dried currants
¼ cup chopped fresh basil
¼ cup chopped fresh parsley
DRESSING
⅓ cup (80ml) olive oil
⅓ cup (80ml) white wine vinegar
1 teaspoon French mustard
1 teaspoon sugar

Add rice to pan of boiling water, boil, uncovered, until tender; drain. Add dressing to hot rice; mix well, cool to room temperature.

Meanwhile, quarter peppers, remove seeds and membranes. Grill peppers, skin side up, until skin blisters and blackens. Peel away skin, cut peppers into strips. Add peppers and remaining ingredients to rice mixture; mix well.

Dressing: Combine all ingredients in jar; shake well.

Serves 4.

- ■ Recipe best made on day of serving.
- ■ Storage: Covered, in refrigerator.
- ■ Freeze: Not suitable.
- ■ Microwave: Rice suitable.

◉ Add 80g sliced pepperoni or salami to salad.

RIGHT: Clockwise from left: Tomato Rice Slice, Rice with Currants and Red Peppers, Saffron Couscous with Raisins and Almonds.

China from Villeroy & Boch.

BAKED POLENTA WITH TWO CHEESES

1.25 litres (5 cups) water
1 vegetable stock cube
2 cups (300g) polenta
400g mozzarella cheese, sliced
100g blue cheese, crumbled

TOMATO SAUCE
1 tablespoon olive oil
2 cloves garlic, crushed
1 medium onion, chopped
2 x 410g cans tomatoes
¼ cup (60ml) tomato paste
1 teaspoon sugar
1 tablespoon chopped fresh oregano

Grease 15cm x 25cm loaf pan. Add water and crumbled stock cube to large pan, bring to boil. Add polenta, simmer, uncovered, about 15 minutes or until polenta is soft, stirring occasionally. Press mixture into prepared pan, cool; refrigerate until cold. Turn polenta out, cut into 1cm slices.

Grease shallow ovenproof dish (2.5 litres/10 cup capacity). Spoon half the tomato sauce into dish, top with over-lapping slices of polenta and mozzarella cheese. Drizzle remaining tomato sauce over polenta, sprinkle with blue cheese. Bake in moderately hot oven about 40 minutes or until browned.

Tomato Sauce: Heat oil in pan, add garlic and onion, cook, stirring, until onion is soft. Add undrained crushed tomatoes, paste, sugar and oregano, simmer, uncovered, until sauce is thickened.

Serves 6.

- ■ Recipe can be made 3 hours ahead.
- ■ Storage: Covered, in refrigerator.
- ■ Freeze: Not suitable.
- ■ Microwave: Tomato sauce suitable.

◉ Serve sprinkled with 6 chopped, cooked bacon rashers.

NUTTY BURGHUL SALAD NICOISE

1 cup (160g) burghul
400g new potatoes, halved
200g green beans, halved
12 chives
6 green shallots
500g cherry tomatoes
8 hard-boiled eggs, quartered
1 cup (170g) small black olives
3 cloves garlic, crushed
2 tablespoons drained
    capers, chopped

DRESSING
¼ cup (60ml) white wine vinegar
½ cup (125ml) extra virgin olive oil
¼ cup (40g) pine nuts, toasted
¼ cup chopped fresh parsley
¼ cup chopped fresh mint

Place burghul in heatproof bowl, cover with boiling water, stand 15 minutes; drain, rinse under cold water, drain. Blot

dry with absorbent paper. Boil, steam or microwave potatoes and beans separately until tender. Cut chives and shallots into 5cm lengths. Combine burghul, potatoes, beans, chives, shallots and remaining ingredients in bowl; add dressing, mix gently.
Dressing: Combine all ingredients in jar; shake well.

Serves 6.

- ■ Recipe can be prepared 3 hours ahead.
- ■ Storage: Covered, in refrigerator.
- ■ Freeze: Not suitable.
- ■ Microwave: Suitable.

 Add 425g can drained tuna to finished salad.

LEFT: From back: Baked Polenta with Two Cheeses, Nutty Burghul Salad Nicoise.
ABOVE: Leek and Rice Flan with Sesame Mushrooms.

LEEK AND RICE FLAN WITH SESAME MUSHROOMS

¾ cup (150g) basmati rice
½ small onion, finely chopped
¼ cup (20g) grated parmesan cheese
1 tablespoon chopped
    fresh coriander
1 egg, lightly beaten
½ teaspoon dried chilli flakes

LEEK FILLING
60g butter
3 large leeks, shredded
1½ tablespoons grated fresh ginger
¼ cup chopped fresh coriander
3 eggs, lightly beaten
1 cup (250ml) cream

SESAME MUSHROOMS
2 teaspoons sesame oil
1 tablespoon vegetable oil
4 cloves garlic, crushed
¼ cup (35g) sesame seeds
600g shitake mushrooms
2 tablespoons light soy sauce
2 tablespoons sake

Grease 24cm flan tin, line base and side with foil, grease foil well. Add rice to pan of boiling water, boil, uncovered, until tender; drain well. Combine rice and remaining ingredients in bowl; mix well. Press mixture evenly over base and side of prepared tin; place tin on oven tray, refrigerate 30 minutes.

Pour leek filling into rice crust. Bake, uncovered, in moderately hot oven about 45 minutes or until browned and firm. Serve topped with sesame mushrooms.
Leek Filling: Heat butter in pan, add leeks, ginger and coriander, cook, stirring, until leeks are soft; cool. Combine leek mixture, eggs and cream in bowl; mix well.
Sesame Mushrooms: Heat oils in pan, add garlic and seeds, cook, stirring, until seeds are lightly browned. Add remaining ingredients, cook, stirring, until mushrooms are soft.

Serves 6.

- ■ Flan can be made a day ahead.
- ■ Storage: Covered, in refrigerator.
- ■ Freeze: Not suitable.
- ■ Microwave: Sesame mushrooms suitable.

● Add ½ cup (100g) chopped, cooked turkey or chicken to leek filling.

TOFU AND RICE SALAD WITH GINGER CRISPS

375g packet tofu, drained
½ cup (90g) wild rice
1 cup (200g) jasmine rice
3 medium zucchini
2 medium carrots
1 medium leek

DRESSING
1 medium orange
⅔ cup (160ml) orange juice
2 teaspoons grated fresh ginger
1½ tablespoons honey
½ teaspoon five spice powder
2 teaspoons light soy sauce
½ teaspoon sesame oil
2 tablespoons hoi sin sauce

GINGER CRISPS
10cm piece (about 80g) fresh ginger
oil for deep-frying
¼ cup (40g) icing sugar mixture

Cut tofu into 1cm cubes. Combine tofu and dressing in bowl, cover, refrigerate several hours or overnight.

Drain tofu, reserve dressing. Add wild rice to pan of boiling water, boil, uncovered, about 35 minutes or until tender, drain. Add jasmine rice to pan of boiling water, boil, uncovered, until tender, drain. Combine rices in bowl.

Cut zucchini, carrots and leek into thin 4cm strips. Add vegetables to pan of boiling water, boil, uncovered, until just tender; drain, rinse under cold water, drain. Combine rices and vegetables in bowl.

Serve drizzled with some of the reserved dressing, top with tofu, ginger crisps and remaining dressing.
Dressing: Using vegetable peeler, peel rind thinly from orange. Cut rind into thin strips, combine with remaining ingredients in bowl.
Ginger Crisps: Using vegetable peeler, peel thin strips of ginger. Deep-fry strips in hot oil until crisp, toss in icing sugar.

Serves 4.

- Tofu can be prepared a day ahead.
- Storage: Covered, in refrigerator.
- Freeze: Not suitable.
- Microwave: Vegetables suitable.

 Substitute 400g sliced Chinese barbecued pork for tofu.

FRESH ASPARAGUS RISOTTO

3 bunches (about 750g)
fresh asparagus
30g butter
2 tablespoons olive oil
3 medium leeks, chopped
3 cloves garlic, crushed
2½ cups (500g) arborio rice
⅔ cup (160ml) dry white wine
3 cups (750ml) vegetable stock
3¾ cups (930ml) water
1 cup (80g) grated parmesan cheese
2 tablespoons chopped fresh parsley
30g butter, extra

Cut asparagus into 2.5cm lengths. Boil, steam or microwave asparagus until just tender; drain, rinse under cold water, drain well.

Heat butter and oil in pan, add leeks and garlic, cook, stirring, until leeks are soft. Add rice, stir until combined.

Combine wine, stock and water in another pan, bring to boil, keep hot.

Stir ⅔ cup (160ml) hot stock mixture into rice mixture, cook, stirring, over low heat until liquid is absorbed. Continue adding stock mixture very gradually, stirring until absorbed before next addition. Total cooking time should be about 30 minutes or until rice is tender. Stir in asparagus, cheese, parsley and extra butter, stir until heated through.

Serves 4 to 6.

- Recipe best made just before serving.
- Freeze: Not suitable.
- Microwave: Asparagus suitable.

⊚ Add 1 cup (150g) chopped, cooked chicken to risotto with asparagus.

BLACK BEAN, RICE AND VEGETABLE PILAF

½ cup (100g) Mexican black turtle beans
1 large red Spanish onion
30g butter
1 teaspoon cumin seeds
1 teaspoon coriander seeds
1 cinnamon stick
6 cardamom pods
3 cloves
1 teaspoon turmeric
1 teaspoon garam masala
1 medium carrot, sliced
1½ cups (300g) long-grain rice
1½ cups (375ml) vegetable stock
1½ cups (375ml) water
1 medium green pepper, chopped

Add beans to pan of boiling water, boil, uncovered, about 40 minutes or until tender; drain.

Cut onion into 8 wedges. Heat butter in large pan, add onion and spices, cook, stirring, about 1 minute or until fragrant. Add carrot and rice, stir until combined. Add stock and water, simmer, covered, 8 minutes, add beans and pepper, simmer, covered, further 2 minutes or until rice is tender and liquid absorbed.

Serves 4 to 6.

- Recipe best made close to serving.
- Freeze: Not suitable.
- Microwave: Not suitable.

⊚ Add 300g chopped, cooked lamb to rice mixture with beans and pepper.

RIGHT: Clockwise from back: Tofu and Rice Salad with Ginger Crisps, Black Bean, Rice and Vegetable Pilaf, Fresh Asparagus Risotto.

Johnson Brothers bowl and oval dish from Waterford Wedgwood Australia Ltd.

CURRIED MILLET PILAF

2 tablespoons vegetable oil
1 medium onion, chopped
2 cloves garlic, crushed
1 teaspoon sambal oelek
1 teaspoon curry powder
1 teaspoon turmeric
2 cups (420g) hulled millet
1 litre (4 cups) vegetable stock
2 medium carrots, chopped
250g cauliflower, chopped
1 medium red pepper, chopped
100g snow peas
¼ cup chopped fresh parsley

Heat oil in pan, add onion, garlic, sambal oelek, spices and millet, cook, stirring, until onion is soft and millet is browned. Stir in stock, carrots, cauliflower and pepper. Stir over heat until mixture boils, simmer, uncovered, about 25 minutes or until vegetables and millet are tender and mixture is thick. Add snow peas, stir over heat until peas are tender; stir in parsley.

Serves 4.

- Recipe best made close to serving.
- Freeze: Not suitable.
- Microwave: Suitable.

Add 500g cooked, sliced steak to pilaf with snow peas.

CHEESE POLENTA WITH MUSHROOM ROSEMARY SAUCE

1 cup (250ml) milk
1½ cups (375ml) vegetable stock
1½ cups (375ml) water
1 cup (150g) polenta
1 cup (80g) coarsely grated parmesan cheese
plain flour
oil for deep-frying

MUSHROOM ROSEMARY SAUCE
100g butter
300g oyster mushrooms, halved
400g Swiss brown mushrooms, halved
300g button mushrooms
2 tablespoons chopped fresh rosemary
¼ cup (60ml) dry white wine
½ cup (125ml) sour cream
2 teaspoons Worcestershire sauce
2 teaspoons Dijon mustard

Grease 19cm x 29cm Swiss roll pan, line base and sides with baking paper. Combine milk, stock and water in large pan, bring to boil, add polenta, stir over heat about 10 minutes or until polenta is soft; stir in cheese. Press mixture into prepared pan, cool, cover, refrigerate until cold.

Turn polenta out, cut into triangles. Toss triangles in flour, shake away excess flour. Deep-fry polenta in hot oil until browned; drain on absorbent paper. Serve with mushroom rosemary sauce.

Mushroom Rosemary Sauce: Heat butter in pan, add mushrooms and rosemary, cook, stirring, 2 minutes. Add remaining ingredients, cook, stirring, until mushrooms are soft.

Serves 4 to 6.

- Polenta can be prepared a day ahead.
- Storage: Covered, in refrigerator.
- Freeze: Unfried polenta, suitable.
- Microwave: Mushroom rosemary sauce suitable.

Replace ½ cup (40g) of the parmesan cheese with 200g chopped ham; add to polenta mixture with cheese.

ABOVE: From left: Curried Millet Pilaf, Cheese Polenta with Mushroom Rosemary Sauce.
RIGHT: From left: Pumpkin and Silverbeet Barley Risotto, Minted Burghul Salad with Cucumber Yogurt.

Above: China from Villeroy & Boch.

PUMPKIN AND SILVERBEET BARLEY RISOTTO

800g pumpkin, peeled
2 tablespoons olive oil
1 medium leek, chopped
1 clove garlic, crushed
1½ cups (300g) pearl barley
½ cup (125ml) dry white wine
3 cups (750ml) vegetable stock
3 cups (750ml) water
½ bunch (about 6 leaves)
  silverbeet, shredded
1 cup (125g) frozen peas, thawed
⅔ cup (50g) grated parmesan cheese

Cut pumpkin into 2cm pieces. Boil, steam or microwave pumpkin until tender, drain. Mash two-thirds of pumpkin, reserve remaining pieces.

Heat oil in pan, add leek and garlic, cook, stirring, until leek is soft, add barley, stir until combined. Add wine, simmer, uncovered, until almost all wine is evaporated. Stir in stock and water, simmer, uncovered, about 40 minutes or until barley is tender, stirring occasionally. Add silverbeet, stir until wilted. Add mashed pumpkin, reserved pumpkin pieces, peas and cheese, stir until heated through.

Serves 4.

■ Recipe best made close to serving.
■ Freeze: Not suitable.
■ Microwave: Suitable.

◉ Top risotto with 100g chopped salami or ham.

MINTED BURGHUL SALAD WITH CUCUMBER YOGURT

2 medium red peppers
2 medium yellow peppers
1 cup (160g) burghul
¼ cup (60ml) olive oil
4 small lady finger eggplants, sliced
4 small zucchini, sliced
200g button mushrooms, halved
⅔ cup chopped fresh mint

DRESSING
½ cup (125ml) olive oil
½ cup (125ml) lemon juice
1 clove garlic, crushed
1 teaspoon sugar

CUCUMBER YOGURT
½ small green cucumber, peeled,
  seeded, chopped
⅔ cup (160ml) plain yogurt

Quarter peppers, remove seeds and membranes. Grill peppers, skin side up, until skin blisters and blackens. Peel away skin, cut peppers into strips.

Place burghul in heatproof bowl, cover with boiling water, stand 15 minutes; drain, rinse under cold water, drain. Blot dry with absorbent paper.

Heat oil in pan or on barbecue plate, add eggplants, zucchini and mushrooms in batches, cook until tender; drain on absorbent paper. Cut eggplants and zucchini into strips.

Combine peppers, burghul, eggplants, zucchini, mushrooms, mint and dressing in bowl; mix well. Serve topped with cucumber yogurt.

Dressing: Combine all ingredients in jar; shake well.

Cucumber Yogurt: Combine cucumber and yogurt in bowl; mix well.

Serves 4.

■ Recipe best made about 3 hours before serving.
■ Storage: Covered, in refrigerator.
■ Freeze: Not suitable.
■ Microwave: Not suitable.

◉ Top salad with 250g sliced, barbecued lamb or beef.

TOMATO BURGHUL WITH SCRAMBLED EGGS

1 cup (160g) burghul
1 tablespoon olive oil
1 medium onion, chopped
2 cloves garlic, crushed
2 x 425g cans tomatoes
2 tablespoons tomato paste
1½ tablespoons sweet chilli sauce
2 tablespoons chopped fresh basil
1 tablespoon chopped fresh oregano
½ vegetable stock cube
⅓ cup (80ml) sour cream
2 tablespoons chopped fresh chives

SCRAMBLED EGGS
20g butter
8 eggs, lightly beaten
⅔ cup (160ml) cream

Place burghul in heatproof bowl, cover with boiling water, stand 15 minutes; drain, rinse under cold water, drain. Blot dry with absorbent paper.

Heat oil in pan, add onion and garlic, cook, stirring, until onion is soft. Add undrained crushed tomatoes, paste, sauce, herbs and crumbled stock cube. Simmer, uncovered, 2 minutes; stir in burghul. Serve topped with scrambled eggs, sour cream and chives.

Scrambled Eggs: Heat butter in pan, add combined eggs and cream, cook, stirring, until mixture is just set.

Serves 4.

■ Recipe best made close to serving.
■ Freeze: Not suitable.
■ Microwave: Scrambled eggs suitable.

◉ Cook half quantity scrambled eggs. Add 500g smoked haddock to pan of simmering water, simmer, uncovered, until just tender; drain. Remove skin, cut fish into strips. Top scrambled eggs with fish.

PINEAPPLE RICE SALAD WITH COCONUT DRESSING

1 cup (200g) long-grain rice
1 cup (200g) brown rice
300g broccoli, chopped
300g cauliflower, chopped
300g snow peas, halved
1 small pineapple, chopped
½ cup (75g) unsalted
    roasted cashews
½ cup (40g) flaked almonds, toasted
½ cup (75g) dried currants

COCONUT DRESSING
2 tablespoons vegetable oil
½ teaspoon ground cumin
½ teaspoon turmeric
¾ cup (180ml) coconut cream
2 tablespoons lemon juice
2 teaspoons sugar
2 tablespoons water

Add rices to separate pans of boiling water, boil, uncovered, until tender; drain,
cool. Boil, steam or microwave broccoli, cauliflower and snow peas separately until just tender; drain, rinse under cold water, drain. Combine rices, vegetables and remaining ingredients in bowl, add coconut dressing; mix well.

Coconut Dressing: Heat oil in pan, add cumin and turmeric, stir until fragrant, remove from heat. Combine spice mixture, coconut cream, juice, sugar and water in bowl; mix well.

Serves 4 to 6.

■ Recipe can be made a day ahead.
■ Storage: Covered, in refrigerator.
■ Freeze: Not suitable.
■ Microwave: Rices and vegetables suitable.

◉ Add 2 cups (300g) chopped, cooked chicken to salad before serving.

CRUNCHY RICE SALAD WITH TOASTED ALMONDS

30g butter
1 medium onion, sliced
1 cinnamon stick
1 teaspoon cumin seeds
6 cardamom pods
1 teaspoon turmeric
1 cup (200g) basmati rice
2 cups (500ml) boiling water
½ cup (70g) slivered
    almonds, toasted
⅓ cup (30g) coconut, toasted
1 medium zucchini, grated
1 stick celery, sliced
¼ cup chopped fresh coriander

Heat butter in pan, add onion, cinnamon, seeds, cardamom and turmeric, cook, stirring, until fragrant. Add rice, cook, stirring, 1 minute. Add water, simmer, covered with tight-fitting lid, about 15 minutes, or until rice is tender and all liquid absorbed; cool. Discard cinnamon and cardamom. Combine rice mixture and remaining ingredients in bowl; mix well.

Serves 4.

■ Recipe best made on day of serving.
■ Storage: Covered, in refrigerator.
■ Freeze: Not suitable.
■ Microwave: Not suitable.

◉ Add 3 chopped, cooked bacon rashers to rice salad with remaining ingredients.

RIGHT: Clockwise from left: Tomato Burghul with Scrambled Eggs, Pineapple Rice Salad with Coconut Dressing, Crunchy Rice Salad with Toasted Almonds.

Johnson Brothers china from Waterford Wedgwood Australia Ltd.

MUSHROOM AND BARLEY CABBAGE ROLLS

8 large cabbage leaves
2/3 cup (130g) pearl barley
2 tablespoons olive oil
1 medium onion, finely chopped
2 cloves garlic, crushed
1/3 cup (50g) pine nuts
1 tablespoon chopped fresh thyme
1 teaspoon grated lemon rind
400g button mushrooms, halved
1/3 cup (50g) dried currants
1/2 teaspoon ground cinnamon
1/2 teaspoon ground nutmeg
1 tablespoon chopped fresh oregano
1/4 cup (15g) stale breadcrumbs
2 cups (500ml) hot vegetable stock
1/4 cup (60ml) dry sherry
30g butter

Boil, steam or microwave cabbage until just wilted, rinse under cold water, drain; pat dry with absorbent paper.

Add barley to pan of boiling water, boil, uncovered, about 40 minutes or until tender; drain.

Heat oil in pan, add onion, garlic, nuts, thyme and rind, cook, stirring, until onion is soft and nuts are lightly browned. Add mushrooms, cook, stirring, until mushrooms are soft. Stir in barley, currants, spices, oregano and breadcrumbs.

Place cabbage leaves on bench, cut away hard cores. Place 1/2 cup (125ml) filling on each leaf, roll up tightly, folding in sides, to enclose filling.

Place cabbage rolls, seam side down, in ovenproof dish, pour over stock. Bake, uncovered, in moderate oven about 30 minutes or until heated through; remove rolls from dish. Add sherry to stock in dish, simmer, uncovered, until reduced by half; stir in butter. Serve cabbage rolls drizzled with stock mixture.

Makes 8.

■ Recipe can be made a day ahead.
■ Storage: Covered, in refrigerator.
■ Freeze: Not suitable.
■ Microwave: Suitable.

◎ Use only 1/3 cup (65g) pearl barley and 200g button mushrooms. Add 400g pork and veal mince to softened onion, cook, stirring, until lightly browned and cooked through.

BURGHUL AND WILD RICE SALAD

2 cups (320g) burghul
⅔ cup (120g) wild rice
2 medium red peppers
200g baby yellow squash, quartered
12 quail eggs
4 green shallots, chopped
⅔ cup (70g) pecans or walnuts
2 tablespoons chopped fresh parsley
2 tablespoons chopped fresh chives

DRESSING
⅔ cup (160ml) olive oil
2 tablespoons lemon juice
1 clove garlic, crushed
½ teaspoon seasoned pepper

Place burghul in heatproof bowl, cover with boiling water, stand 15 minutes; drain, rinse under cold water, drain. Blot dry with absorbent paper.

Add rice to pan of boiling water, boil, uncovered, about 35 minutes or until rice is tender; drain, rinse under cold water, drain.

Quarter peppers, remove seeds and membranes. Grill peppers, skin side up, until skin blisters and blackens. Peel away skin, cut peppers into thin strips. Add squash to pan of boiling water, simmer, uncovered, until squash are tender; drain, rinse under cold water, drain.

Place eggs in pan, cover with cold water, simmer, uncovered, 4 minutes; drain, rinse under cold water. Remove shells, cut eggs in half.

Combine burghul, rice, peppers, squash, shallots, nuts and herbs in bowl. Top salad with eggs, drizzle with dressing.
Dressing: Combine all ingredients in jar; shake well.
Serves 4 to 6.

- ■ Recipe can be made several hours ahead.
- ■ Storage: Covered, in refrigerator.
- ■ Freeze: Not suitable.
- ■ Microwave: Rice and squash suitable.

◉ Replace quail eggs with 4 quail. Cut quail into quarters, barbecue or grill until tender. Top salad with quail.

LEEK POLENTA WITH BABY BEETS

50g butter
3 medium leeks, chopped
2 cloves garlic, crushed
1 litre (4 cups) vegetable stock
1½ cups (225g) polenta
¼ cup chopped fresh thyme
1 egg yolk
1 cup (80g) grated parmesan cheese
¼ cup (30g) grated fontina cheese
20g butter, melted, extra
24 baby beetroot
150g snow peas
½ bunch (about 325g)
**   English spinach**
80g snow pea sprouts
3 green shallots, chopped

MUSTARD DRESSING
2 teaspoons Dijon mustard
1 tablespoon seeded mustard
2 tablespoons red wine vinegar
½ teaspoon sugar
⅔ cup (160ml) olive oil
¼ cup chopped fresh basil

Grease 20cm x 30cm lamington pan, cover base with baking paper. Heat butter in pan, add leeks and garlic, cook, stirring, until leeks are soft.

Bring stock to boil in pan, add polenta gradually, cook, stirring, about 10 minutes or until thick and soft; cool slightly. Stir in leek mixture, thyme, egg yolk and half the combined cheeses; mix well. Press mixture into prepared pan, cover, refrigerate about 2 hours or until firm.

Turn polenta onto board, cut out 6 x 9cm rounds. Place rounds on greased oven tray, brush with extra butter, sprinkle with remaining cheeses. Bake in moderately hot oven about 20 minutes or until browned.

Trim beetroot, reserve 12 leaves. Boil, steam or microwave beetroot until tender, peel. Combine beetroot and half the mustard dressing in bowl.

Boil, steam or microwave snow peas until just tender; drain, rinse under cold water, drain. Combine reserved beetroot leaves, snow peas, spinach leaves, sprouts and shallots in bowl, pour over remaining dressing; mix gently. Serve warm polenta rounds with warm beetroot and salad.
Mustard Dressing: Combine all ingredients in jar; shake well.
Serves 6.

- ■ Polenta can be prepared a day ahead.
- ■ Storage: Covered, in refrigerator.
- ■ Freeze: Not suitable.
- ■ Microwave: Beetroot and snow peas suitable.

◉ Add 160g ham or sliced, grilled pancetta to salad.

ABOVE LEFT: From left: Burghul and Wild Rice Salad; Mushroom and Barley Cabbage Rolls.
RIGHT: Leek Polenta with Baby Beets.

Above left: Bowls from Primex Products; salad servers from Jarass Pty Ltd.
Right: China from Accoutrement.

POTATO AND BURGHUL BALLS WITH PLUM SAUCE

You will need about 2 large (550g) old potatoes and about 180g kumara.

½ cup (80g) burghul
2 cups cold cooked mashed potato
⅔ cup cold cooked mashed kumara
⅓ cup (50g) plain flour
1 teaspoon five spice powder
1 egg, lightly beaten
2 cups (140g) stale breadcrumbs
plain flour, extra
1 cup (160g) burghul, extra
oil for deep-frying

SWEET ONION FILLING
1 tablespoon vegetable oil
1 medium red Spanish
   onion, chopped
1 medium onion, chopped
2 teaspoons sugar
2 teaspoons sweet chilli sauce
2 teaspoons light soy sauce
1½ tablespoons dried currants
1½ tablespoons pine nuts

PLUM SAUCE
⅓ cup (80ml) plum sauce
3 teaspoons hoi sin sauce
⅓ cup (80ml) dry sherry
2 teaspoons honey

Place burghul in heatproof bowl, cover with boiling water, stand 15 minutes; drain, rinse under cold water, drain. Blot dry with absorbent paper.

Combine burghul, potato, kumara, flour, spice powder, egg and breadcrumbs in bowl. Drop level tablespoons of mixture in extra flour, roll into balls, flatten slightly.

Spoon 1 teaspoon of sweet onion filling in centre of half the flattened balls, top with remaining flattened balls, press edges to seal. Toss in extra burghul, roll into balls.

Deep-fry balls in batches in hot oil until browned and heated through, drain on absorbent paper. Serve with plum sauce.

Sweet Onion Filling: Heat oil in pan, add onions, cook, covered, over low heat, stirring occasionally, about 15 minutes or until very soft. Add remaining ingredients, stir until well combined.

Plum Sauce: Combine all ingredients in bowl; mix well.

Makes about 25.

■ Uncooked filled balls and sauce can be prepared a day ahead.
■ Storage: Covered, separately, in refrigerator.
■ Freeze: Not suitable.
■ Microwave: Not suitable.

RICE AND MUSHROOM TIMBALES WITH SALAD

¼ cup (45g) wild rice
30g butter
1 cup (200g) long-grain rice
3 cups (750ml) water
2 vegetable stock cubes
4 sprigs fresh flat-leafed parsley

MUSHROOM FILLING
30g butter
1 medium onion, finely chopped
1 clove garlic, crushed
¼ cup (60ml) dry white wine
150g button mushrooms, sliced
150g oyster mushrooms, chopped
¾ cup (180ml) cream

SALAD
1 bunch rocket
1 small Spanish onion, thinly sliced
1 medium red pepper, thinly sliced
½ cup (125ml) extra virgin olive oil
¼ cup (60ml) cider vinegar
1 clove garlic, crushed
2 teaspoons seeded mustard
1 tablespoon chopped fresh mint

Add wild rice to pan of boiling water, boil, uncovered, about 35 minutes or until tender; drain.

Heat butter in pan, add long-grain rice, stir until coated with butter. Stir in water and crumbled stock cubes, boil, uncovered, about 5 minutes or until almost all liquid is evaporated. Cook, covered, over low heat 10 minutes. Remove from heat, stand 5 minutes. Stir in wild rice.

Lightly grease 4 ovenproof moulds (1 cup/250ml capacity). Cover bases with greaseproof paper. Place a sprig of parsley on base of each mould. Divide rice mixture into 4 portions. Press three-quarters of each portion over base and side of each mould. Spoon mushroom filling evenly into moulds, top with remaining rice mixture, press lightly; cover with foil.

Place in baking dish with enough boiling water to come halfway up sides of moulds. Bake in moderate oven 30 minutes. Stand 5 minutes before turning onto serving plates. Serve with salad.

Mushroom Filling: Heat butter in pan, add onion and garlic, cook, stirring, until onion is soft. Stir in wine and mushrooms, then cream, cook, stirring, until thickened, remove from heat; cool.

Salad: Combine rocket, onion and pepper in bowl, add combined oil, vinegar, garlic, mustard and mint; mix gently.

Serves 4.

■ Mushroom filling can be made a day ahead.
■ Storage: Covered, in refrigerator.
■ Freeze: Not suitable.
■ Microwave: Wild rice suitable.

● Cut 400g squid hoods into thin strips, stir-fry until just tender. Combine squid with salad.

ARTICHOKES WITH WILD RICE SEASONING

8 fresh medium globe artichokes
1½ cups (375ml) water
1 cup (250ml) dry white wine
½ cup (125ml) olive oil
2 tablespoons lemon juice
2 cloves garlic, crushed
6 sprigs fresh thyme

WILD RICE SEASONING
**1 cup (200g) wild rice/brown
    rice blend**
2 tablespoons olive oil
1 medium onion, chopped
2 cloves garlic, crushed
**½ cup (70g) drained sun-dried
    capsicums, chopped**
⅓ cup chopped fresh oregano
¼ cup (40g) pine nuts, toasted
2 teaspoons olive paste
1 tablespoon drained chopped capers
⅓ cup (25g) grated romano cheese

ROCKET SALAD
1 medium radicchio lettuce
1 bunch rocket
**1 cup firmly packed fresh flat-leafed
    parsley leaves**
1½ tablespoons balsamic vinegar
⅓ cup (80ml) extra virgin olive oil

Remove tough outer leaves from artichokes, trim tips of remaining leaves. Pull away some inside leaves, scoop out coarse centre with spoon. Peel stem, trim to 5cm. Combine water, wine, oil, juice, garlic and thyme in large pan, bring to boil, add artichokes, simmer, covered, about 20 minutes or until tender. Drain artichokes, discard cooking liquid. Cut artichokes in half lengthways, fill with wild rice seasoning. Serve with rocket salad.

Wild Rice Seasoning: Add rice to pan of boiling water, boil, uncovered, about 35 minutes or until tender; drain, rinse under cold water, drain. Heat oil in pan, add onion and garlic, cook, stirring, until soft.

Stir in rice and remaining ingredients.

Rocket Salad: Combine torn radicchio leaves, rocket and parsley in bowl; drizzle with combined vinegar and oil.

Serves 4.

- ■ Artichokes and wild rice seasoning can be prepared a day ahead.
- ■ Storage: Covered, separately, in refrigerator.
- ■ Freeze: Not suitable.
- ■ Microwave: Rice suitable.

⦿ Add 70g chopped prosciutto to wild rice seasoning.

LEFT: Potato and Burghul Balls with Plum Sauce.
ABOVE: From left: Artichokes with Wild Rice Seasoning, Rice and Mushroom Timbales with Salad.

Left: Plate from Primex Products. Above: Pottery from Kenwick Galleries.

Pasta

Easy and satisfying meals with pasta are enjoyable to cook, and always very popular. There are many shapes, sheets, strips and tubes to buy; use what you prefer, provided it suits the recipe. We also tell you how to make fresh pasta, using the simplest ingredients. Our recipes are scrumptiously different, with temptations such as dainty open herb lasagne with beetroot and spinach, cheesy baked gnocchi with tomato sauce and olives, peppered pasta with vegetables and gremolata, and hearty, wholemeal pasta pie with pizza-style topping. The symbol ◉ indicates a variation, if desired.

●

WHOLEMEAL LASAGNE WITH RATATOUILLE AND BEANS

1 small eggplant, chopped
coarse cooking salt
2 tablespoons olive oil
1 medium onion, chopped
2 cloves garlic, crushed
2 medium zucchini, chopped
1 medium red pepper, chopped
100g baby yellow squash, quartered
425g can tomatoes
1 teaspoon sugar
310g can 4 bean mix, rinsed, drained
2 tablespoons chopped fresh oregano
2 tablespoons tomato paste
6 instant wholemeal lasagne sheets
¼ cup (15g) stale breadcrumbs
¼ cup (20g) grated parmesan cheese

WHITE SAUCE
60g butter
½ cup (75g) plain flour
2½ cups (625ml) milk
1 egg, lightly beaten
¼ cup (20g) grated parmesan cheese

Grease ovenproof dish (1.75 litre/7 cup capacity). Sprinkle eggplant with salt, stand 30 minutes. Rinse eggplant under cold water, pat dry with absorbent paper.

Heat oil in pan, add onion and garlic, cook, stirring, until onion is soft. Add eggplant, zucchini, pepper and squash, cook, stirring, until vegetables are just tender. Add undrained crushed tomatoes, sugar, bean mix, oregano and paste, simmer, covered, about 10 minutes or until thickened slightly.

Cover base of prepared dish with 3 lasagne sheets, spread with half the vegetable mixture, top with half the white sauce. Repeat with remaining lasagne, vegetable mixture and white sauce. Sprinkle with combined breadcrumbs and cheese. Place on oven tray, bake, uncovered, in moderate oven about 45 minutes or until browned.

White Sauce: Melt butter in pan, add flour, cook, stirring, until bubbling. Remove from heat, gradually stir in milk, stir over heat until sauce boils and thickens. Cool 2 minutes; stir in egg and cheese.

Serves 6.

■ Recipe can be made a day ahead.
■ Storage: Covered, in refrigerator.
■ Freeze: Not suitable.
■ Microwave: White sauce suitable.

RIGHT: From left: Linguine with Creamy Asparagus, Wholemeal Lasagne with Ratatouille and Beans.

China from Villeroy & Boch.

LINGUINE WITH CREAMY ASPARAGUS

2 bunches (about 500g)
fresh asparagus
1 medium red Spanish onion
1 tablespoon olive oil
150g sugar snap peas
½ cup (55g) drained sun-dried tomatoes, sliced
300ml sour cream
½ cup (125ml) cream
1 tablespoon seeded mustard
200g linguine pasta
1 tablespoon chopped fresh chives
⅓ cup (25g) parmesan cheese flakes

Cut asparagus into 4cm lengths. Cut onion into thin wedges. Heat oil in pan, add asparagus, onion and peas, cook, stirring, until onion is just tender. Add tomatoes, creams and mustard, simmer, uncovered, until slightly thickened. Add pasta to pan of boiling water, boil, uncovered, until just tender; drain. Add pasta and chives to asparagus mixture, stir until combined. Serve topped with cheese.

Serves 4 to 6.

■ Recipe best made close to serving.
■ Freeze: Not suitable.
■ Microwave: Pasta suitable.

◉ Add 300g thinly sliced, pan-fried veal fillet and 4 rashers chopped, cooked bacon to asparagus mixture.

SPINACH, CHEESE AND TOMATO GNOCCHI

²⁄₃ bunch (420g) English spinach
1kg ricotta cheese
2 cups (160g) grated
    parmesan cheese
4 eggs, lightly beaten
½ teaspoon ground nutmeg
1½ cups (225g) plain flour
2 tablespoons tomato paste

TOMATO OLIVE SAUCE
2 tablespoons olive oil
2 medium onions, sliced
3 cloves garlic, sliced
½ cup (125ml) dry red wine
2 x 425g cans tomatoes
⅓ cup (80ml) tomato paste
¾ cup (180ml) vegetable stock
1 teaspoon sugar
½ cup (90g) baby black olives
⅓ cup chopped fresh basil

Boil, steam or microwave spinach until wilted, drain, rinse under cold water; drain. Squeeze spinach dry, chop finely.

Combine cheeses, eggs, nutmeg and flour in bowl; mix well. Divide mixture into 3 portions. Add spinach to 1 portion; mix well. Add tomato paste to another portion; mix well. Leave remaining portion plain.

Using floured hands, roll level tablespoons of plain mixture into ovals, toss ovals in flour. Place an oval in palm of hand, press floured fork onto dough to make indentations and flatten slightly. Repeat with remaining mixtures.

Add gnocchi to pan of boiling water, boil, uncovered, about 2 minutes or until tender; drain well. Serve gnocchi with tomato olive sauce.

Tomato Olive Sauce: Heat oil in pan, add onions and garlic, cook, stirring, until onions are soft. Add wine, simmer, uncovered, until almost all liquid is evaporated. Stir in undrained crushed tomatoes, paste, stock, sugar and olives, simmer, uncovered, until slightly thickened, stir in basil.

Serves 6.

■ Gnocchi and tomato olive sauce can be prepared a day ahead.
■ Storage: Covered, separately, in refrigerator.
■ Freeze: Gnocchi suitable.
■ Microwave: Gnocchi and spinach suitable.

◉ Add 180g chopped pepperoni or salami to sauce.

SESAME NOODLE AND VEGETABLE SALAD

10 (20g) Chinese dried mushrooms
500g fresh thick egg noodles
6 baby eggplants
oil for deep-frying
150g snow peas, halved
½ bunch (about 270g) Chinese broccoli, chopped
2 cups (100g) watercress sprigs
80g snow pea sprouts
70g oyster mushrooms
½ medium red pepper, sliced
½ medium yellow pepper, sliced
2 green shallots, sliced
¼ cup (35g) sesame seeds, toasted
¼ cup chopped fresh coriander

DRESSING
¼ cup (60ml) sweet chilli sauce
⅓ cup (80ml) light soy sauce
¼ cup (60ml) balsamic vinegar
1½ tablespoons sugar
1½ tablespoons sesame oil
⅓ cup (80ml) vegetable oil

Place mushrooms in heatproof bowl, cover with boiling water, stand 20 minutes. Drain mushrooms, discard stems, slice mushrooms. Add noodles to pan of boiling water, boil until just tender; drain, rinse under cold water; drain. Cut eggplants lengthways into 5mm slices, deep-fry in hot oil until lightly browned; drain on absorbent paper.

Boil, steam or microwave snow peas and broccoli separately until just tender; drain, rinse under cold water, drain.

Toss watercress in a little of the dressing, place on plate. Combine noodles, eggplants, snow peas, broccoli, dried mushrooms, sprouts, oyster mushrooms, peppers, shallots, seeds and coriander in bowl, pour over remaining dressing; mix well. Top watercress with noodle salad.
Dressing: Combine all ingredients in jar; shake well.

Serves 6.

- Recipe best made just before serving.
- Freeze: Not suitable.
- Microwave: Noodles, snow peas and broccoli suitable.

◉ Mix 2 cups (300g) chopped Chinese barbecued duck or barbecued chicken through salad.

OPEN HERB LASAGNE WITH BEETROOT AND SPINACH

⅔ cup (100g) plain flour
1 egg
1 teaspoon olive oil
⅓ cup fresh flat-leafed parsley leaves
4 small fresh beetroot
2 tablespoons olive oil, extra
1 clove garlic, crushed
1 medium leek, sliced
6 beetroot leaves, coarsely shredded
10 English spinach leaves, coarsely shredded
2 tablespoons chopped walnuts

DRESSING
⅓ cup (80ml) olive oil
⅓ cup (80ml) white wine vinegar
2 tablespoons walnut oil
1 teaspoon sugar
1 teaspoon Dijon mustard
2 cloves garlic, crushed

Process flour, egg and oil until combined. Turn dough onto floured surface, knead until smooth. Cover, refrigerate 30 minutes.

Roll dough through thickest setting on pasta machine until smooth and elastic. Divide pasta in half, roll each half through pasta machine ending at second thinnest setting.

Brush 1 side of parsley leaves with a little water, place parsley, water side down, on 1 piece of pasta, lightly brush remaining pasta with water, place over parsley, press gently to seal. Roll pasta once through second thinnest setting of machine. Cut pasta into 12 squares.

Add pasta to large pan of boiling water, simmer, uncovered, about 2 minutes or until just tender; drain, rinse under cold water, drain. Brush each side of pasta with dressing, keep between layers of baking paper until needed.

Boil, steam or microwave beetroot until just tender; drain, peel, slice. Heat extra oil in pan, add garlic and leek, cook, stirring, until leek is soft. Add beetroot leaves and spinach, cook, stirring, until leaves are just wilted.

Layer 3 squares of pasta on a plate with some of the beetroot and spinach mixture; drizzle with dressing, sprinkle with nuts. Repeat with remaining ingredients.
Dressing: Blend or process all ingredients until smooth and creamy.

Serves 4.

- Recipe can be prepared a day ahead.
- Storage: Covered, separately, in refrigerator.
- Freeze: Uncooked pasta suitable.
- Microwave: Pasta and beetroot suitable.

◉ Divide 16 fresh oysters between serving plates.

ABOVE LEFT: From left: Spinach, Cheese and Tomato Gnocchi, Sesame Noodle and Vegetable Salad.
RIGHT: Open Herb Lasagne with Beetroot and Spinach.

Above left: China from Villeroy & Boch; wire basket from Linen & Lace of Balmain. Right: Plate from Primex Products.

CHEESE AND SPINACH CANNELLONI

1 tablespoon olive oil
1 medium onion, chopped
2 cloves garlic, crushed
1 bunch (about 650g) English
spinach, shredded
¼ cup chopped fresh basil
2 tablespoons chopped fresh oregano
3 cups (600g) ricotta cheese
¼ cup (20g) grated parmesan cheese
¼ cup (20g) flaked almonds
250g packet (24) cannelloni shells
½ cup (40g) grated parmesan
cheese, extra

TOMATO SAUCE
1 tablespoon olive oil
1 medium onion, chopped
1 clove garlic, crushed
2 x 410g cans tomatoes
1 teaspoon sugar

Grease large shallow ovenproof dish (3 litre/12 cup capacity). Heat oil in pan, add onion and garlic, cook, stirring, until onion is soft. Add spinach and herbs, cook, stirring, until spinach is wilted and excess liquid evaporated; cool. Stir in cheeses and nuts.

Spoon spinach mixture into piping bag without tube, pipe into cannelloni shells. Place shells in single layer in prepared dish, pour over tomato sauce. Bake, uncovered, in moderate oven 30 minutes, sprinkle with extra cheese; bake further 10 minutes or until cheese is melted.
Tomato Sauce: Heat oil in pan, add onion and garlic, cook, stirring, until onion is soft. Add undrained crushed tomatoes and sugar, simmer, uncovered, about 10 minutes or until thickened.

Serves 6.

■ Recipe can be made a day ahead.
■ Storage: Covered, in refrigerator.
■ Freeze: Suitable.
■ Microwave: Tomato sauce suitable.

◉ Use 1½ cups (300g) ricotta cheese, omit almonds; replace with 1 cup (200g) finely chopped, cooked chicken in filling.

SPAGHETTI WITH TOMATO BEAN SAUCE

2 tablespoons olive oil
3 cloves garlic, crushed
425g can tomatoes
⅔ cup (160ml) tomato puree
½ cup (125ml) water
1 teaspoon sugar
1 teaspoon chopped fresh oregano
1 teaspoon chopped fresh thyme
310g can cannellini beans,
rinsed, drained
¼ cup (40g) pitted black olives, sliced
500g spaghetti pasta

Heat oil in pan, add garlic, cook 30 seconds. Add undrained crushed tomatoes, puree, water, sugar and herbs, simmer, uncovered, until sauce is thickened slightly. Stir in beans and olives, stir over heat until heated through.

Add pasta to large pan of boiling water, boil, uncovered, until just tender; drain. Serve pasta with tomato bean sauce.

Serves 4.

■ Sauce can be made a day ahead.
■ Storage: Covered, in refrigerator.
■ Freeze: Sauce suitable.
■ Microwave: Pasta suitable.

◉ Add 425g can drained tuna to sauce with beans.

BAKED GNOCCHI WITH TOMATO SAUCE AND OLIVES

3 cups (750ml) milk
1 teaspoon salt
pinch ground nutmeg
⅔ cup (110g) semolina
1 egg, lightly beaten
1½ cups (120g) grated
parmesan cheese
40g butter, melted
⅓ cup (55g) pitted black olives, sliced

TOMATO SAUCE
1 tablespoon olive oil
1 medium onion, finely chopped
2 cloves garlic, crushed
425g can tomatoes
2 tablespoons tomato paste
¼ cup (60ml) dry red wine
1 teaspoon sambal oelek
1 tablespoon chopped fresh oregano
1 tablespoon chopped fresh thyme
¼ cup shredded fresh basil

Lightly oil 23cm square cake pan. Combine milk, salt and nutmeg in pan, bring to boil, reduce heat, gradually stir in semolina, stir over heat about 10 minutes or until mixture is thick. Remove from heat, stir in egg and 1 cup (80g) of the cheese. Spread mixture into prepared pan, cover, refrigerate 1 hour.

Turn gnocchi out of pan, cut into 4cm rounds. Cover oven tray with baking paper. Place rounds over-lapping on tray, brush with butter, sprinkle with remaining cheese. Bake, uncovered, in moderate oven about 15 minutes or until lightly browned. Serve topped with tomato sauce, sprinkle with olives.
Tomato Sauce: Heat oil in pan, add onion and garlic, cook, stirring, until onion is soft. Add undrained crushed tomatoes, paste, wine, sambal oelek and herbs, simmer, uncovered, about 5 minutes or until sauce is thickened slightly.

Serves 4.

■ Tomato sauce can be made a day ahead.
■ Storage: Covered, in refrigerator.
■ Freeze: Not suitable.
■ Microwave: Tomato sauce suitable.

◉ Serve 500g barbecued or grilled baby octopus with gnocchi.

ABOVE: Clockwise from top: Cheese and Spinach Cannelloni, Baked Gnocchi with Tomato Sauce and Olives, Spaghetti with Tomato Bean Sauce.

China, glasses and tray from Home & Garden on the Mall.

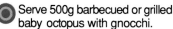

FENNEL AND TOMATO RAVIOLI WITH GARLIC OIL

2 cups (300g) plain flour
1 tablespoon chopped fennel bulb
3 eggs, lightly beaten
2 teaspoons olive oil
¾ cup (60g) parmesan cheese flakes

FILLING
2 tablespoons olive oil
60g butter
½ medium fennel bulb,
finely chopped
1 small leek, finely chopped
¼ cup (35g) finely chopped drained
sun-dried tomatoes

GARLIC OIL
1 medium onion
½ cup (125ml) olive oil
2 cloves garlic, sliced
1 small fresh red chilli, sliced

Process flour, fennel, eggs and oil until combined. Turn dough onto floured surface, press ingredients together; knead until smooth. Cover, refrigerate 30 minutes.

Cut dough into 4 pieces. Roll out 1 piece until 1mm thick. Place 2 level teaspoons of filling about 6cm apart over pasta. Roll out another portion until 1mm thick, lightly brush with water, place over filling; press firmly between filling. Cut into large rectangular ravioli shapes, lightly sprinkle with flour. Repeat with remaining dough and filling.

Add ravioli to pan of boiling water,

simmer, uncovered, about 5 minutes or until tender; drain. Serve ravioli drizzled with garlic oil and sprinkled with cheese.
Filling: Heat oil and butter in pan, add fennel and leek, cook, covered, over low heat about 20 minutes or until fennel is soft; stir in tomatoes.
Garlic Oil: Cut onion into 8 wedges. Heat oil in pan, add onion, garlic and chilli, cook, stirring, until onion is soft.

Serves 8 as an entree.

■ Uncooked filled ravioli and garlic oil can be made a day ahead.
■ Storage: Covered, separately, in refrigerator.
■ Freeze: Not suitable.
■ Microwave: Ravioli suitable.

◉ Add 70g chopped salami to garlic oil with onion.

PEPPERED PASTA WITH VEGETABLES AND GREMOLATA

2 cups (300g) plain flour
3 eggs
1 tablespoon chopped fresh thyme
1 tablespoon chopped fresh oregano
1 teaspoon cracked
black peppercorns
2 teaspoons olive oil
3 medium red peppers
2 medium carrots
2 medium green zucchini
1 medium yellow zucchini
1 large leek
80g butter
¼ cup (60ml) cream
1 cup (80g) grated parmesan cheese
½ cup (80g) pine nuts, toasted

GREMOLATA
2 teaspoons grated lemon rind
1 cup chopped fresh parsley
2 cloves garlic, crushed

Process flour, eggs, herbs, peppercorns and oil until combined. Turn dough onto floured surface, knead until smooth. Cover, refrigerate 1 hour.

Cut dough into 4 pieces, roll 1 piece through pasta machine set on thickest setting. Fold dough in half, roll through machine. Repeat rolling and folding several times until dough is thin and elastic. Roll dough through machine, adjusting setting, roll until second thinnest setting. Using pastry wheel, cut long strips of pasta 2.5cm wide, toss in some extra flour. Repeat with remaining dough pieces.

Add pasta in batches to large pan of boiling water, simmer about 2 minutes or until tender; drain.

Quarter peppers, remove seeds and membranes. Grill peppers, skin side up, until skin blisters and blackens. Peel away skin, cut peppers into 2cm strips.

Using vegetable peeler, peel long thin strips from carrots and zucchini. Cut leek into long strips, 2cm wide. Boil, steam or microwave carrots, zucchini and leek until just tender; drain. Heat butter and cream in pan, stir until combined.

Combine hot pasta with peppers, carrots, zucchini, leek, butter mixture, half the cheese, half the nuts and half the gremolata in bowl, toss to combine. Sprinkle with remaining cheese, nuts and gremolata.

Gremolata: Combine all ingredients in bowl; mix well.

Serves 4.

■ Recipe best made just before serving.
■ Freeze: Not suitable.
■ Microwave: Carrots, zucchini, leek and pasta suitable.

 Add 500g sliced, cooked veal fillets to pasta mixture with vegetables.

CURRIED CAULIFLOWER WITH SPINACH PASTA

30g butter
1 medium onion, thinly sliced
1 small red pepper, sliced
1 teaspoon cumin seeds
3 teaspoons curry powder
1 tablespoon plain flour
1½ cups (375ml) milk
1 cup (250ml) water
500g cauliflower, chopped
300g spinach fettuccine pasta
¼ cup (40g) pine nuts, toasted

Heat butter in pan, add onion, pepper and cumin seeds, cook, stirring, until onion is soft. Add curry powder and flour, cook, stirring, until grainy. Remove from heat, gradually stir in combined milk and water. Stir over heat until mixture boils and thickens. Add cauliflower, simmer, covered, until cauliflower is just tender.

Add pasta to large pan of boiling water, boil, uncovered, until just tender; drain. Serve cauliflower mixture over pasta, sprinkle with nuts.

Serves 4.

■ Cauliflower mixture can be made a day ahead.
■ Storage: Covered, in refrigerator.
■ Freeze: Not suitable.
■ Microwave: Suitable.

 Add 4 sliced, pan-fried lamb fillets to cauliflower mixture before serving.

LEFT: From left: Fennel and Tomato Ravioli with Garlic Oil, Peppered Pasta with Vegetables and Gremolata.
ABOVE: Curried Cauliflower with Spinach Pasta.

Left: China from Corso de Fiori. Above: Plate, cloth and glasses are Christopher Vine Design.

PENNE WITH ZUCCHINI CREAM

4 medium zucchini
45g butter
1 medium onion, thinly sliced
1 clove garlic, crushed
300ml cream
½ cup (125ml) milk
300g penne pasta
¾ cup (60g) grated parmesan cheese
¾ cup shredded fresh basil

Cut zucchini in half lengthways, cut diagonally into 5mm slices. Heat butter in pan, add onion and garlic, cook, stirring, until onion is soft. Add zucchini, cook, stirring, 1 minute. Stir in cream and milk, simmer, uncovered, 1 minute.

Add pasta to large pan of boiling water, boil, uncovered, until just tender; drain. Add pasta, cheese and basil to zucchini mixture, stir until combined.

Serves 4.

■ Recipe best made just before serving.
■ Freeze: Not suitable.
■ Microwave: Pasta suitable.

◉ Add 600g cooked, peeled medium prawns to zucchini mixture with pasta.

CRISP RICE NOODLES WITH STIR-FRIED VEGETABLES

80g rice vermicelli noodles
oil for deep-frying
¼ cup (60ml) vegetable oil
1 teaspoon sesame oil
2 medium zucchini, sliced
2 sticks celery, sliced
1 medium yellow pepper, chopped
1 medium red pepper, chopped
1 medium carrot, sliced
150g button mushrooms, halved

ORANGE GINGER SAUCE
1½ cups (375ml) orange juice
⅓ cup (80ml) light soy sauce
½ cup (125ml) mirin
⅓ cup (80ml) sake
½ cup (125ml) green ginger wine
½ cup (125ml) honey

Deep-fry noodles in hot oil in batches until puffed and crisp; drain on absorbent paper.

Heat 1 tablespoon combined vegetable oil and sesame oil in pan or wok, add vegetables, stir-fry in batches until lightly browned, adding more oil mixture as needed; drain. Serve with noodles and orange ginger sauce.

Orange Ginger Sauce: Combine all ingredients in pan, simmer, uncovered, about 10 minutes or until thickened.

Serves 4.

■ Recipe best made just before serving.
■ Freeze: Not suitable.
■ Microwave: Not suitable.

◉ Cook 500g piece of rump steak in pan after cooking vegetables. Slice steak thinly, before serving.

FETTUCCINE WITH FRESH BEETROOT

2 bunches (about 12) baby beetroot
1 tablespoon olive oil
1 large onion, chopped
1 clove garlic, crushed
1 vegetable stock cube
⅔ cup (160ml) dry white wine
300ml cream
125g packet cream cheese, chopped
500g plain fettuccine pasta
⅔ cup (50g) grated parmesan cheese

Trim leaves from beetroot, reserve leaves. Boil, steam or microwave beetroot until tender. Peel away skin; cut beetroot in half. Shred beetroot leaves.

Heat oil in pan, add onion and garlic, cook, stirring, until onion is soft. Add beetroot leaves, stir until just wilted. Add crumbled stock cube, wine and cream, simmer, uncovered, about 5 minutes or until thickened slightly. Add cream cheese, stir until melted.

Add pasta to large pan of boiling water, boil, uncovered, until just tender; drain. Combine pasta, parmesan cheese and sauce; mix well. Serve pasta topped with beetroot.

Serves 6.
■ Recipe best made close to serving.
■ Freeze: Not suitable.
■ Microwave: Pasta and beetroot suitable.

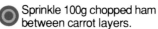 Add 60g sliced prosciutto or ham to pan with onion and garlic.

CARROT AND FETA CHEESE LASAGNE

50g butter
1 tablespoon olive oil
2 medium leeks, chopped
3 cloves garlic, crushed
8 medium (about 1kg) carrots, grated
½ cup shredded fresh basil
4 eggs, lightly beaten
300ml cream
1 teaspoon seasoned pepper
6 sheets instant lasagne pasta
400g feta cheese, crumbled

Grease 17cm x 25cm ovenproof dish (2 litre/8 cup capacity). Heat butter and oil in pan, add leeks and garlic, cook, stirring, until leeks are soft. Add carrots, cook, covered, stirring occasionally, about 10 minutes or until carrots are soft; cool slightly, stir in basil. Combine eggs, cream and pepper in bowl; mix well.

Cover base of prepared dish with half the lasagne sheets, top with half the carrot mixture, half the cheese and half the egg mixture. Repeat layers, finishing with egg mixture. Bake, uncovered, in moderate oven about 50 minutes or until firm and browned.

Serves 4 to 6.
■ Recipe can be made a day ahead.
■ Storage: Covered, in refrigerator.
■ Freeze: Not suitable.
■ Microwave: Not suitable.

Sprinkle 100g chopped ham between carrot layers.

LEFT: From left: Penne with Zucchini Cream, Crisp Rice Noodles with Stir-Fried Vegetables.
ABOVE: From left: Fettuccine with Fresh Beetroot, Carrot and Feta Cheese Lasagne.

Left: China from Villeroy & Boch.
Above: Glassware and plates are Christopher Vine Design.

MINTED PASTA MOULDS WITH TOMATO VINAIGRETTE

1 cup (190g) stellini pasta
2/3 cup (70g) frozen broad beans
2/3 cup (80g) frozen peas
2 tablespoons chopped fresh chives
1/4 cup shredded fresh mint
150g feta cheese, crumbled

SALAD
1 red oak leaf lettuce
100g snow pea sprouts
1/2 medium red pepper, sliced
1 small green cucumber, chopped

TOMATO VINAIGRETTE
4 medium tomatoes, peeled, seeded, chopped
2 tablespoons white vinegar
1/4 cup (60ml) olive oil
1/4 teaspoon French mustard
1/2 teaspoon sugar

Grease 6 moulds (1/2 cup/125ml capacity). Add pasta to large pan of boiling water, boil, uncovered, until just tender; drain (do not rinse). Boil, steam or microwave beans and peas until just tender; drain. Remove skins from beans.

Combine hot pasta, beans, peas and remaining ingredients in bowl. Divide mixture evenly between prepared moulds, press mixture firmly into moulds. Stand 5 minutes before turning onto plates. Serve with salad and tomato vinaigrette.
Salad: Combine torn lettuce and remaining ingredients in bowl.
Tomato Vinaigrette: Process all ingredients until smooth.

Serves 6 as an entree.

■ Moulds can be made a day ahead.
■ Storage: Covered, in refrigerator.
■ Freeze: Not suitable.
■ Microwave: Suitable.

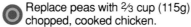 Replace peas with 2/3 cup (115g) chopped, cooked chicken.

CRISP AVOCADO RAVIOLI WITH WATERCRESS SAUCE

1 small avocado, finely chopped
1/2 small onion, finely chopped
2 teaspoons lemon juice
2 teaspoons sweet chilli sauce
200g packet frozen gow gees pastry wrappers, thawed
1 egg, lightly beaten
oil for deep-frying

WATERCRESS SAUCE
30g butter
2 green shallots, chopped
3 cups (about 100g) watercress sprigs, firmly packed
1 teaspoon seeded mustard
1 vegetable stock cube
1/2 cup (125ml) water
1 teaspoon lemon juice
1/2 cup (125ml) cream

PASTA WITH CURRANTS AND PINE NUTS

2 tablespoons olive oil
2 cloves garlic, crushed
2 medium onions, finely chopped
1 cinnamon stick
2 teaspoons ground cumin
2 teaspoons ground coriander
1 teaspoon garam masala
310g can chick peas, rinsed, drained
250g cherry tomatoes, halved
1/3 cup (50g) dried currants
1/3 cup (80ml) olive oil, extra
500g penne pasta
1/3 cup (50g) pine nuts, toasted
1/4 cup shredded fresh basil

Heat oil in pan, add garlic and onion, cook, stirring, until onions are soft. Add spices, cook, stirring, until fragrant. Add chick peas, tomatoes, currants and extra oil, stir until combined and heated through.

Add pasta to large pan of boiling water, boil, uncovered, until just tender; drain. Combine sauce and pasta in bowl; sprinkle with nuts and basil.

Serves 4.

■ Recipe best made just before serving.
■ Freeze: Not suitable.
■ Microwave: Pasta suitable.

◉ Add 300g sliced, stir-fried squid hoods or chicken to pasta with chick peas.

CHILLI CHEESY PASTA WITH GARLIC CRUMBS

1 small yellow pepper
1/3 cup (80ml) olive oil
1/2 teaspoon dried chilli flakes
2 cloves garlic, crushed
1 1/2 cups (105g) stale breadcrumbs
500g spinach fettuccine pasta
2 eggs, lightly beaten
1/2 cup (40g) grated parmesan cheese
100g smoked cheese, grated
2 teaspoons chopped fresh oregano
1/3 cup (80ml) cream

Cut pepper into thin strips. Heat oil in pan, add pepper, chilli, garlic and breadcrumbs, cook, stirring, until pepper is soft and crumbs are well browned.

Add pasta to large pan of boiling water, boil, uncovered, until just tender; drain. Add combined eggs, cheeses, oregano and cream to pasta in bowl; mix well. Top with breadcrumb mixture.

Serves 4.

■ Breadcrumb mixture can be made 3 hours ahead.
■ Storage: Covered, in refrigerator.
■ Freeze: Not suitable.
■ Microwave: Pasta suitable.

LEFT: Clockwise from top left: Crisp Avocado Ravioli with Watercress Sauce, Pasta with Currants and Pine Nuts, Minted Pasta Moulds with Tomato Vinaigrette.
BELOW: Chilli Cheesy Pasta with Garlic Crumbs.

Left: China from Villeroy & Boch. Below: Pasta plate from Hale Imports.

Combine avocado, onion, juice and sauce in bowl; mix well. Brush edge of 1 pastry wrapper with egg, place 2 level teaspoons of avocado mixture in centre, fold pastry over to enclose filling; seal edge with fork. Repeat with remaining pastry, egg and avocado mixture. Deep-fry ravioli in hot oil until browned; drain. Serve ravioli with watercress sauce.

Watercress Sauce: Heat butter in pan, add shallots, cook, stirring, until soft. Add watercress, cook, stirring, over high heat until watercress is wilted. Add mustard, crumbled stock cube, water and juice, simmer, uncovered, 1 minute. Blend or process mixture until smooth. Return mixture to pan, add cream, stir until heated through.

Serves 4.

■ Recipe best made just before serving.
■ Freeze: Not suitable.
■ Microwave: Sauce suitable.

◉ Serve with flesh from 1 flaked, smoked trout or 500g shelled prawns.

EGGPLANT AND MUSHROOM PASTITSO

1 medium eggplant
2 tablespoons olive oil
1 tablespoon olive oil, extra
1 medium onion, chopped
2 cloves garlic, crushed
200g button mushrooms, halved
2 x 410g cans tomatoes
½ cup (125ml) dry red wine
1½ cups (375ml) vegetable stock
250g penne pasta
1½ cups (185g) grated tasty cheese
pinch ground nutmeg

CREAM SAUCE
2 cups (400g) ricotta cheese, sieved
3 eggs, lightly beaten
1 cup (250ml) cream
¾ cup (90g) grated tasty cheese
⅓ cup (25g) grated parmesan cheese

Cut eggplant into 2cm pieces. Heat oil in pan, add eggplant, cook until lightly browned; drain on absorbent paper. Add extra oil to same pan, add onion, garlic and mushrooms, cook, stirring, until onion is soft.

Combine undrained crushed tomatoes, wine and stock in another pan, simmer, uncovered, stirring occasionally, about 10 minutes or until thick. Stir in eggplant and mushroom mixture.

Add pasta to large pan of boiling water, boil, uncovered, until just tender; drain. Combine pasta with half the eggplant mixture. Spread into large ovenproof dish (2.5 litre/10 cup capacity). Top with remaining eggplant mixture, spread with cream sauce, sprinkle with cheese and nutmeg. Bake, uncovered, in moderate oven about 40 minutes or until heated through and browned.

Cream Sauce: Combine all ingredients in bowl; mix well.

Serves 4 to 6.

- Recipe can be made a day ahead.
- Storage: Covered, in refrigerator.
- Freeze: Not suitable.
- Microwave: Pasta suitable.

PASTA WITH CARAMELISED ONIONS AND BEANS

60g butter
3 medium red Spanish onions, sliced
¼ cup (60ml) water
⅓ cup (65g) brown sugar
½ cup (125ml) brown vinegar
¼ cup (55g) raisins
300g green beans, halved
500g spaghetti pasta
1 tablespoon olive oil
2 cloves garlic, crushed
1 bunch (about 650g) English
    spinach, shredded

Heat butter in pan, add onions and water, cook, covered, over low heat about 15 minutes, stirring occasionally, or until onions are soft. Add sugar, vinegar and raisins, cook, covered, further 15 minutes.

Boil, steam or microwave beans until just tender; drain.

Add pasta to large pan of boiling water, boil, uncovered, until just tender; drain. Combine pasta and half the onion mixture in bowl; mix well.

Heat oil in pan, add garlic, spinach and beans, cook, stirring, until spinach is just wilted and beans are heated through. Serve pasta mixture topped with spinach mixture and remaining onion mixture.

Serves 4.

- Recipe best made just before serving.
- Freeze: Not suitable.
- Microwave: Beans and pasta suitable.

  ◉ Add 1 pan-fried, sliced pork fillet to pasta with onion mixture.

LEFT: From left: Pasta with Caramelised Onions and Beans, Eggplant and Mushroom Pastitso.
ABOVE: Tagliatelle with Radicchio Cream Sauce.

Above: Green raffia placemat and basket from Morris Home & Garden Wares.

TAGLIATELLE WITH RADICCHIO CREAM SAUCE

3 medium leeks
oil for deep-frying
400g thin tagliatelle pasta
60g butter
4 cloves garlic, crushed
½ cup (125ml) dry white wine
1 cup (250ml) vegetable stock
2 (about 200g) radicchio
    lettuce, shredded
300ml cream
⅓ cup shredded fresh basil
⅓ cup (25g) romano cheese flakes

Trim leeks to 15cm long. Cut leeks into very thin strips lengthways. Deep-fry half the leeks in hot oil until lightly browned and crisp; drain on absorbent paper.

Add pasta to large pan of boiling water, boil, uncovered, until just tender; drain.

Heat butter in pan, add remaining leeks and garlic, cook, stirring, until leeks are soft. Add wine and stock, simmer, uncovered, until reduced by half. Stir in lettuce, cream and basil, simmer until lettuce is wilted and hot. Toss cream sauce through pasta, top with cheese and deep-fried leeks.

Serves 4.

- Recipe best made close to serving.
- Freeze: Not suitable.
- Microwave: Pasta suitable.

  ◉ Top leeks with 125g sliced, cooked prosciutto or chopped ham.

71

MUSHROOM RICOTTA RAVIOLI WITH TOMATO SAUCE

2 tablespoons olive oil
1 small onion, chopped
1 clove garlic, crushed
250g flat mushrooms, finely chopped
2 tablespoons grated
** parmesan cheese**
⅔ cup (130g) ricotta cheese
200g packet frozen gow gees pastry
** wrappers, thawed**
½ cup (40g) grated parmesan
** cheese, extra**

TOMATO SAUCE
1 tablespoon olive oil
1 small onion, sliced
1 clove garlic, crushed
410g can tomatoes
⅓ cup (80ml) dry red wine
1 teaspoon sugar
2 tablespoons shredded fresh basil

Heat oil in pan, add onion and garlic, cook, stirring, until onion is soft. Add mushrooms, cook, stirring, further 5 minutes or until mushrooms are tender and liquid evaporated. Transfer mixture to bowl, stir in both cheeses; mix well.

Place 2 level teaspoons mushroom mixture on centre of each pastry wrapper. Brush edges lightly with water, fold in half to enclose filling; press edges firmly.

Add ravioli to large pan of boiling water, boil, uncovered, about 2 minutes or until just tender; drain. Serve ravioli with tomato sauce and extra cheese.

Tomato Sauce: Heat oil in pan, add onion and garlic, cook, stirring, until onion is soft. Stir in undrained crushed tomatoes, wine and sugar, simmer, uncovered, until thickened slightly; stir in basil.

Serves 4.

■ Recipe best made close to serving.
■ Freeze: Not suitable.
■ Microwave: Ravioli suitable.

⦿ Substitute 125g cooked, minced beef for ricotta cheese in filling.

WHOLEMEAL PASTA WITH PEPPERS AND ARTICHOKES

1½ cups (185g) frozen peas
2 medium red peppers
⅔ cup (160ml) olive oil
2 cloves garlic, crushed
6 green shallots, chopped
8 artichoke hearts in oil,
** drained, halved**
500g wholemeal tagliatelle pasta
¼ cup shredded fresh basil
1 cup (80g) parmesan cheese flakes

Add peas to pan of boiling water, simmer, uncovered, until tender; drain.

Quarter peppers, remove seeds and membranes. Grill peppers, skin side up, until skin blisters and blackens. Peel away skin, cut peppers into thin strips.

Heat oil in pan, add garlic and shallots, cook, stirring, until shallots are soft. Stir in peas, peppers and artichokes, stir until hot.

Add pasta to large pan of boiling water, simmer, uncovered, until tender; drain. Combine hot pasta with pepper mixture and basil, top with cheese.

SPINACH PASTA WITH CREAMY KUMARA SAUCE

You will need about 20 English spinach leaves for this recipe.

**¼ cup drained chopped
  cooked spinach**
2 cups (300g) plain flour
2 eggs

CREAMY KUMARA SAUCE
2 tablespoons olive oil
250g kumara, grated
1 clove garlic, crushed
1 cup (250ml) cream
½ cup (125ml) dry white wine
⅓ cup (25g) grated parmesan cheese
2 teaspoons Dijon mustard

KUMARA CHIPS
200g kumara
oil for deep-frying

Squeeze excess moisture from spinach. Process spinach, flour and eggs until ingredients form a ball. Turn dough onto floured surface, knead until smooth. Cut dough in half, roll each half through pasta machine set on thickest setting. Fold dough in half, roll through machine. Repeat folding and rolling several times until dough is smooth and elastic. Roll dough through machine, adjusting setting to become less thick with each roll, dusting with extra flour when necessary. Roll dough through fettuccine attachment of machine.

Add pasta to large pan of boiling water, simmer, uncovered, about 3 minutes or until tender; drain. Serve creamy kumara sauce over pasta; top with kumara chips.
Creamy Kumara Sauce: Heat oil in pan, add kumara and garlic, cook, stirring, 2 minutes. Add remaining ingredients, simmer, uncovered, until sauce is slightly thickened and kumara is tender.
Kumara Chips: Using vegetable peeler, peel long strips from kumara. Deep-fry strips in hot oil until lightly browned and crisp; drain on absorbent paper.

Serves 6 as an entree.

■ Kumara chips can be made
  a week ahead.
■ Storage: Airtight container.
■ Freeze: Not suitable.
■ Microwave: Pasta suitable.

◉ Add 100g finely chopped ham to
  creamy kumara sauce.

Serves 4.

■ Recipe best made just before serving.
■ Freeze: Not suitable.
■ Microwave: Pasta suitable.

◉ Add 200g sliced ham, cut into thin
  strips, to pepper mixture.

ABOVE: From left: Wholemeal Pasta with Peppers and Artichokes, Mushroom Ricotta Ravioli with Tomato Sauce.
RIGHT: Spinach Pasta with Creamy Kumara Sauce.

Right: Bowls and glassware from Home & Garden on the Mall.

FETTUCCINE WITH TOMATO AND FENNEL SAUCE

90g butter
1 medium fennel bulb, thinly sliced
1 medium onion, sliced
2 x 410g cans tomatoes
½ cup (125ml) water
2 tablespoons tomato paste
2 teaspoons fennel seeds
1 tablespoon chopped fresh sage
¼ cup (60ml) dry red wine
1 teaspoon sugar
500g spinach fettuccine pasta
1 cup (80g) parmesan cheese flakes

Heat butter in pan, add fennel and onion, cook, stirring, until fennel is soft. Add undrained crushed tomatoes, water, paste, seeds, sage, wine and sugar, simmer, uncovered, until sauce is thickened.

Add pasta to large pan of boiling water, boil, uncovered, until just tender. Serve tomato and fennel sauce over pasta; top with cheese.

Serves 4.

■ Sauce can be made a day ahead.
■ Storage: Covered, in refrigerator.
■ Freeze: Sauce suitable.
■ Microwave: Suitable.

◉ Add 200g sliced pancetta or ham to fennel and onion in pan.

CREAMY VEGETABLE AND SWEET CHILLI PASTA

250g spiral pasta
2 medium carrots
3 sticks celery
1 medium red pepper
1 medium yellow pepper
1 medium red Spanish onion
1 tablespoon vegetable oil
2 cloves garlic, crushed
300ml cream
300ml sour cream
1 tablespoon brown sugar
2 teaspoons sambal oelek
½ teaspoon seasoned pepper
1 tablespoon lime juice
3 green shallots, chopped
⅓ cup (25g) parmesan cheese flakes

Add pasta to large pan of boiling water, boil, uncovered, until just tender; drain. Cut carrots, celery and peppers into thin strips. Cut onion into thin wedges.

Heat oil in large pan, add garlic, carrots, celery, peppers and onion, cook, stirring, until onion is just tender. Add creams, sugar, sambal oelek, pepper and juice to vegetable mixture. Cook, stirring, until mixture is slightly thickened. Stir in pasta and shallots; mix well. Serve topped with cheese.

Serves 6.

■ Recipe best made close to serving.
■ Freeze: Not suitable.
■ Microwave: Pasta suitable.

◉ Add 150g sliced, smoked salmon to pasta with cream mixture.

RISONI AND CORIANDER SALAD

4 eggs, lightly beaten
2½ cups (500g) risoni
5 medium (about 500g) zucchini
1 tablespoon vegetable oil
¾ cup (120g) blanched almonds
1 teaspoon cracked
    black peppercorns
2 teaspoons white mustard seeds
1 teaspoon dried fenugreek
1 teaspoon coriander seeds
½ teaspoon cardamom seeds

DRESSING
2 limes
⅓ cup (75g) sugar
½ cup (125ml) water
½ cup (125ml) white vinegar
2 cloves garlic, crushed
1 teaspoon sambal oelek
½ cup chopped fresh coriander

Pour enough of the beaten eggs to cover base of heated greased pan, cook until lightly browned underneath. Turn omelette, brown other side. Repeat with remaining beaten eggs. Cool omelettes, cut into thin strips.

Add risoni to pan of boiling water, boil, uncovered, until just tender; drain, rinse

under cold water, drain. Cut zucchini into thin strips. Heat oil in pan, add zucchini and remaining ingredients, cook, stirring, 2 minutes; cool. Combine omelette strips, risoni and zucchini mixture in bowl, add dressing; mix well.

Dressing: Using vegetable peeler, peel rind thinly from 1 lime. Cut rind into very thin strips. Squeeze 2 tablespoons juice from limes. Combine rind, juice, sugar, water, vinegar, garlic and sambal oelek in pan, stir over low heat, without boiling, until sugar is dissolved, boil, uncovered, 2 minutes; cool. Stir in coriander.

Serves 6.
- ■ Recipe can be made 3 hours ahead.
- ■ Storage: Covered, in refrigerator.
- ■ Freeze: Not suitable.
- ■ Microwave: Risoni suitable.

- ◎ Add 500g sliced, pan-fried pork fillets to salad with dressing.

LEFT: Fettuccine with Tomato and Fennel Sauce.
ABOVE: From top: Creamy Vegetable and Sweet Chilli Pasta, Risoni and Coriander Salad.

Left: Pottery from Kenwick Galleries. Above: Plates from Cambur Industries Pty Ltd; serviette from Corso de Fiori.

WHOLEMEAL PASTA PIE

8 drained artichokes, halved
1/4 cup (40g) pitted black olives
1/4 cup shredded fresh basil
2 1/2 cups (250g) grated
    mozzarella cheese
1/4 cup (20g) grated parmesan cheese

PASTA BASE
250g wholemeal spiral pasta
40g butter
2 tablespoons plain flour
1 cup (250ml) milk
1 egg, lightly beaten

TOMATO SAUCE
1 tablespoon olive oil
1 medium onion, chopped
2 cloves garlic, crushed
425g can tomatoes
1/4 cup (60ml) tomato paste
1/2 teaspoon sugar

Oil 2cm-deep 28cm pizza pan. Press pasta base firmly over base of prepared dish. Spread with tomato sauce, top with artichokes, olives, basil and cheeses. Bake in hot oven about 20 minutes or until browned.

Pasta Base: Add pasta to pan of boiling water, boil, uncovered, until just tender; drain. Melt butter in pan, add flour, cook, stirring, until bubbling. Remove from heat, gradually stir in milk, stir over heat until mixture boils and thickens. Combine pasta, milk mixture and egg in bowl.

Tomato Sauce: Heat oil in pan, add onion and garlic, cook, stirring, until onion is soft. Add undrained crushed tomatoes, paste and sugar; simmer, uncovered, about 10 minutes or until thick.

Serves 4.

■ Recipe can be made a day ahead.
■ Storage: Covered, in refrigerator.
■ Freeze: Uncooked pie suitable.
■ Microwave: Pasta and tomato
   sauce suitable.

◎ Add 56g can drained anchovies to topping with artichokes.

PASTA WITH MUSHROOMS AND PEPPERCORN BRIE

200g peppercorn brie cheese
60g butter
6 green shallots, chopped
2 cloves garlic, crushed
300g button mushrooms, sliced
200g flat mushrooms, sliced
1/2 cup (125ml) dry white wine
1 cup (250ml) vegetable stock
1 tablespoon seeded mustard
1/4 cup (25g) drained sun-dried
    tomatoes, sliced
1 cup (250ml) cream
2 teaspoons chopped fresh thyme
400g tagliatelle pasta

Remove rind from cheese, slice cheese thinly. Heat butter in pan, add shallots, garlic and both mushrooms, cook, stirring, until mushrooms are soft. Add wine and stock, simmer, uncovered, until liquid is reduced by half. Add mustard, tomatoes, cheese, cream and thyme, stir until cheese is melted.

Add pasta to pan of boiling water, boil, uncovered, until just tender; drain, serve with sauce.

Serves 4.

■ Recipe best made close to serving.
■ Freeze: Not suitable.
■ Microwave: Pasta suitable.

◎ Add 600g cooked, peeled prawns to sauce with cheese.

*LEFT: From top: Wholemeal Pasta Pie,
Pasta with Mushrooms and Peppercorn Brie.*

China from Corso de Fiori.

Pulses

Peas, beans and lentils are all pulses, or seeds from the pods of certain leguminous plants. They are unobtrusive stars, easy to use, a source of protein and fibre, wonderfully filling and economical, too. In our glossary, we picture the pulses we have used in this section. They show their style in hearty main meals, pretty salads, dinner party fare, casual lunches and snacks, all with lots of colour and great taste. Often we have blended various grains and pulses together for variety and texture. If using dried beans, split peas and chick peas, etc., you generally need to soak them overnight, so allow for this in your planning. The symbol ◉ indicates a variation, if desired.

MEXICAN BROAD BEAN BURGERS

1 tablespoon olive oil
2 medium red Spanish onions, sliced
6 hamburger buns
½ x 450g can refried beans
1 medium avocado, thinly sliced
½ cup (125ml) sour cream
½ cup (125ml) mild chilli sauce

BROAD BEAN PATTIES
½ cup (100g) pearl barley
1kg frozen broad beans
1 medium onion, grated
1¾ cups (120g) stale breadcrumbs
2 eggs
1 tablespoon milk
100g cheese-flavoured corn chips,
    finely crushed

SALSA
1 medium ripe tomato, finely chopped
1 small red Spanish onion,
    finely chopped
1 tablespoon chopped
    fresh coriander
1 tablespoon lime juice
1 teaspoon sugar

Heat oil in pan, add onions, cook, stirring, until soft. Split and toast buns. Fill buns with broad bean patties, heated beans, avocado, salsa, onions, sour cream and chilli sauce.

Broad Bean Patties: Add barley to pan of boiling water, boil, uncovered, about 40 minutes or until tender; drain. Pour boiling water over beans in heatproof bowl, stand 2 minutes; drain. Remove skins from beans, blend or process beans until smooth. Combine barley, bean puree, onion, 1 cup of the breadcrumbs and 1 of the eggs in bowl; mix well.

Shape mixture into 6 patties, dip in combined remaining egg and milk, press on combined corn chips and remaining breadcrumbs. Place patties on greased oven tray, cover, refrigerate 1 hour. Bake in moderately hot oven about 25 minutes or until firm.

Salsa: Combine all ingredients in bowl; mix well.

Makes 6.

■ Patties can be prepared a day ahead.
■ Storage: Covered, in refrigerator.
■ Freeze: Uncooked patties suitable.
■ Microwave: Not suitable.

◉ Cook 6 halved bacon rashers with onions in pan; layer bacon in buns with onions.

RIGHT: Mexican Broad Bean Burgers.

CHICK PEA FRITTATA WITH AVOCADO SALSA

1 tablespoon olive oil
1 medium onion, finely chopped
1 clove garlic, crushed
2 x 310g cans chick peas, rinsed, drained
8 eggs, lightly beaten
2 tablespoons chopped fresh coriander
1 tablespoon chopped fresh parsley

AVOCADO SALSA

1 medium avocado, chopped
1 medium red Spanish onion, finely chopped
2 medium tomatoes, chopped
2 teaspoons chilli sauce

Heat oil in 25cm pan, add onion and garlic, cook, stirring, until onion is soft, stir in chick peas.

Pour combined eggs and herbs over chick pea mixture; mix well. Cook about 10 minutes on medium heat or until set around edges. Grill about 3 minutes or until browned and just set. Turn onto plate, serve with avocado salsa.

Avocado Salsa: Combine all ingredients in bowl; mix well.

Serves 4 to 6.

■ Recipe best made just before serving.
■ Freeze: Not suitable.
■ Microwave: Not suitable.

◉ Add 150g sliced, corned beef to chick pea mixture.

SPICY SPLIT PEA RISOTTO

1 cup (200g) yellow split peas
2 tablespoons olive oil
1 large onion, chopped
2 cloves garlic, crushed
1 teaspoon ground ginger
1 teaspoon garam masala
1 teaspoon ground cumin
½ teaspoon turmeric
pinch chilli powder
3 medium tomatoes, peeled, chopped
1 large potato, chopped
½ cup (100g) brown long-grain rice
2¼ cups (560ml) water
1 vegetable stock cube
2 tablespoons lemon juice
¼ cup chopped fresh coriander

CHICK PEA AND EGGPLANT TIMBALES

2 large eggplants
1/3 cup (80ml) vegetable oil
1 tablespoon vegetable oil, extra
2 cloves garlic, crushed
4 green shallots, chopped
2 teaspoons ground cumin
1/2 teaspoon garam masala
125g packet cream cheese
1/4 cup (60ml) cream
3 eggs
2 x 310g cans chick peas,
**   rinsed, drained**

RED PEPPER PUREE
2 medium red peppers
1 tablespoon olive oil
2 teaspoons white vinegar

Grease 4 ovenproof moulds (1 cup/250ml capacity).

Cut eggplants into 3mm slices, brush with oil. Place eggplant slices in single layer on oven trays, grill on both sides until lightly browned. Line base and side of prepared moulds with eggplant slices, allowing slices to overhang edges.

Heat extra oil in pan, add garlic, shallots, cumin and garam masala, cook, stirring, until fragrant; cool.

Beat cream cheese in small bowl with electric mixer until smooth, add cream and eggs, beat until well combined. Stir in shallot mixture and chick peas; mix well.

Divide mixture between prepared moulds, fold eggplant over to cover filling. Place moulds in baking dish, pour in enough boiling water to come halfway up sides of moulds. Bake, uncovered, in moderate oven about 50 minutes or until firm. Turn onto serving plates, serve with red pepper puree.

Red Pepper Puree: Quarter peppers, remove seeds and membranes. Grill peppers, skin side up, until skin blisters and blackens. Peel away skin. Puree three-quarters of the peppers with oil and vinegar until smooth. Chop remaining pepper, stir into puree.

Serves 4.

- Recipe can be made a day ahead.
- Storage: Covered, separately, in refrigerator.
- Freeze: Not suitable.
- Microwave: Not suitable.

Omit 1 can of chick peas; replace with 250g cooked, minced beef.

LEFT: From top: Chick Pea Frittata with Avocado Salsa, Spicy Split Pea Risotto. BELOW: Chick Pea and Eggplant Timbales.

Left: Striped plate and bowl from Accoutrement; mortar and pestle from Country Furniture Antiques.

Place peas in bowl, cover well with cold water, cover, stand overnight.

Drain peas. Heat oil in pan, add onion, garlic and spices, cook, stirring, until onion is soft. Add tomatoes, potato and rice, cook, stirring, 2 minutes. Add water, crumbled stock cube and juice, simmer, covered, 30 minutes.

Add peas, simmer, covered, further 1 hour or until peas are tender and most of the liquid is absorbed. Stir in coriander.

Serves 4.

- Peas must be prepared a day ahead.
- Storage: Covered, room temperature.
- Freeze: Not suitable.
- Microwave: Not suitable.

Add 300g poached, flaked, smoked fish just before serving.

LENTIL BURGERS WITH ROASTED ONION SALAD

2 cups (400g) red lentils
2 tablespoons vegetable oil
1 medium onion, finely chopped
1 tablespoon grated fresh ginger
2 cloves garlic, crushed
2 teaspoons ground coriander
2 teaspoons ground cumin
3 teaspoons curry powder
1 medium carrot, grated
1 stick celery, finely chopped
1 vegetable stock cube
¼ cup chopped fresh coriander
2 cups (140g) stale breadcrumbs
2 eggs, lightly beaten
½ cup (50g) packaged breadcrumbs
oil for shallow-frying

ROASTED ONION SALAD
8 spring onions, quartered
2 tablespoons olive oil
1 small fresh red chilli, finely chopped
1 clove garlic, sliced
1 teaspoon black mustard seeds
1 teaspoon coriander seeds
250g cherry tomatoes
½ cup fresh mint leaves

Add lentils to pan of boiling water, boil, uncovered, about 8 minutes or until tender; drain. Squeeze excess liquid from lentils. Process half the lentils until smooth, reserve remaining lentils.

Heat oil in pan, add onion, ginger and garlic, cook, stirring, until onion is soft. Add ground coriander and spices, stir over heat until fragrant. Add carrot, celery and crumbled stock cube, cook, stirring, until carrot is soft. Combine lentil puree, reserved lentils, carrot mixture, fresh coriander and 1½ cups of the stale breadcrumbs in bowl; mix well.

Divide mixture into 8 patties. Toss patties in a little flour, dip into eggs then combined remaining stale and packaged breadcrumbs. Shallow-fry patties in hot oil until lightly browned; drain on absorbent paper. Serve with roasted onion salad.

Roasted Onion Salad: Combine onions, oil, chilli, garlic and seeds in ovenproof dish. Bake, covered, in moderate oven 15 minutes. Bake, uncovered, further 10 minutes, add tomatoes and mint, bake, uncovered, further 10 minutes.

Serves 8.

■ Lentil burgers can be prepared a day ahead.
■ Storage: Covered, in refrigerator.
■ Freeze: Not suitable
■ Microwave: Not suitable.

LEFT: From left: Lentil Burgers with Roasted Onion Salad, Chick Pea Salad with Lemon Grass Dressing.
RIGHT: Stir-Fried Mushrooms, Beans and Bok Choy.

Left: Bowl and plate from Corso de Fiori.

CHICK PEA SALAD WITH LEMON GRASS DRESSING

500g broccoli, chopped
300g snow peas
3 medium carrots
150g rice vermicelli noodles
2 x 310g cans chick peas, rinsed, drained
2 tablespoons fresh coriander leaves

LEMON GRASS DRESSING
½ cup (125ml) lime juice
¼ cup (50g) brown sugar
2 stems fresh lemon grass, thinly sliced
1 teaspoon sambal oelek
2 tablespoons vegetable oil

Boil, steam or microwave broccoli and snow peas separately until just tender; drain, rinse under cold water, drain. Using vegetable peeler, peel thin strips from carrots.

Add noodles to large pan of boiling water, boil, uncovered, until just tender; drain, rinse under cold water, drain. Combine broccoli, snow peas, carrots, noodles, chick peas and coriander in bowl, drizzle with dressing; mix well.

Lemon Grass Dressing: Blend or process all ingredients until combined; strain.

Serves 4.

■ Recipe can be prepared 3 hours ahead.
■ Storage: Covered, in refrigerator.
■ Freeze: Not suitable.
■ Microwave: Broccoli, snow peas and noodles suitable.

◉ Add 500g cooked, peeled, medium prawns to salad.

STIR-FRIED MUSHROOMS, BEANS AND BOK CHOY

1 teaspoon sesame oil
1 tablespoon vegetable oil
1 bunch (about 650g) bok choy, coarsely shredded
½ medium Chinese cabbage, coarsely shredded
450g broccoli, chopped
100g shitake mushrooms, halved
150g oyster mushrooms, halved
310g can red kidney beans, rinsed, drained
⅓ cup (80ml) hoi sin sauce
¼ cup (60ml) lime juice
¼ cup (60ml) orange juice

Heat oils in wok or pan, add bok choy and cabbage, stir-fry until just wilted. Add broccoli, mushrooms, beans, sauce and juices, cook, covered, about 3 minutes or until broccoli is tender.

Serves 4.

■ Recipe best made just before serving.
■ Freeze: Not suitable.
■ Microwave: Not suitable.

◉ Add 16 shelled, fresh oysters to pan just before serving.

FENNEL AND LENTIL AU GRATIN

1 cup (200g) brown lentils
2 large fennel bulbs, quartered
1 tablespoon olive oil
1 medium onion, finely chopped
2 cloves garlic, crushed
2 x 410g cans tomatoes
1 tablespoon chopped fresh oregano
1 tablespoon chopped fresh thyme
1 tablespoon chopped fresh basil
½ cup (125ml) dry red wine
1 cup (70g) stale breadcrumbs
½ cup (40g) grated parmesan cheese

WHITE SAUCE
30g butter
2 tablespoons plain flour
1½ cups (375ml) milk
½ cup (125ml) cream
½ cup (60g) grated tasty cheese

Add lentils to pan of boiling water, boil, uncovered, about 15 minutes or until tender; drain, rinse, drain. Add fennel to pan of boiling water, simmer, uncovered, about 15 minutes or until tender; drain.

Heat oil in pan, add onion and garlic, cook until onion is soft. Add undrained crushed tomatoes, herbs and wine, simmer, uncovered, about 15 minutes or until thick; stir in lentils.

Place half the lentil mixture in ovenproof dish (2.5 litre/10 cup capacity), top with fennel and remaining lentil mixture. Pour over white sauce, sprinkle with combined breadcrumbs and cheese. Bake, uncovered, in moderate oven about 40 minutes or until lightly browned.

White Sauce: Melt butter in pan, add flour, cook, stirring, until bubbling. Remove from heat, gradually stir in milk and cream. Stir over heat until sauce boils and thickens, stir in cheese.

Serves 6.

■ Recipe can be made 3 hours ahead.
■ Storage: Covered, in refrigerator.
■ Freeze: Not suitable.
■ Microwave: Fennel suitable.

● Omit ⅓ cup (65g) uncooked lentils; replace with 1 cup (150g) chopped, cooked chicken.

GLAZED PUMPKINS WITH RED LENTIL DRESSING

3 medium (900g) golden
    nugget pumpkins
10 spring onions, halved
80g butter, chopped
1 tablespoon olive oil
2 tablespoons brown sugar
80g feta cheese

RED LENTIL DRESSING
2 tablespoons red lentils
2 teaspoons brown sugar
1½ tablespoons white vinegar
1½ tablespoons orange juice
1 teaspoon Dijon mustard
¼ cup (60ml) olive oil

Cut pumpkins into quarters, remove seeds. Combine pumpkin, onions, butter and oil in large baking dish, bake, uncovered, in moderate oven 50 minutes, turning occasionally. Sprinkle with sugar, bake further 10 minutes.

Serve pumpkin and onion mixture topped with crumbled cheese; drizzle with red lentil dressing.

Red Lentil Dressing: Add lentils to pan of boiling water, boil, uncovered, 8 minutes; drain. Combine lentils, sugar, vinegar, juice and mustard in pan, stir over heat until sugar is dissolved. Add oil, stir until heated through.

Serves 6.

- ■ Recipe can be prepared 3 hours ahead.
- ■ Storage: Covered, room temperature.
- ■ Freeze: Not suitable.
- ■ Microwave: Not suitable.

SPICED CHICK PEAS WITH PARSNIPS AND KUMARA

1½ cups (300g) dried chick peas
2 large onions
300g kumara
3 medium parsnips
¼ cup (60ml) olive oil
2 cloves garlic, crushed
1 teaspoon grated fresh ginger
1 teaspoon coriander seeds
1 teaspoon dried red chilli flakes
1 teaspoon ground cumin
1 teaspoon turmeric
½ teaspoon ground cinnamon
425g can tomatoes
½ teaspoon sugar
½ cup (125ml) water
2 tablespoons tomato paste

Place chick peas in bowl, cover well with cold water, cover, stand overnight.

Add chick peas to large pan of boiling water, boil, uncovered, about 30 minutes or until tender; drain. Cut onions into 8 wedges. Cut kumara and parsnips into 2½cm pieces.

Heat oil in pan, add onions, garlic,

ginger, seeds and spices, cook, stirring, until onions are soft. Add kumara, parsnips and undrained crushed tomatoes, simmer, covered, 20 minutes. Add chick peas, sugar, water and paste, simmer, covered, further 15 minutes or until vegetables are tender.

Serves 4.

- ■ Chick peas best prepared a day ahead.
- ■ Storage: Covered, room temperature.
- ■ Freeze: Not suitable.
- ■ Microwave: Not suitable.

● Add 300g sausages to onions and spices in pan.

LEFT: Fennel and Lentil au Gratin.
ABOVE: From left: Spiced Chick Peas with Parsnips and Kumara, Glazed Pumpkins with Red Lentil Dressing.

Left: China and glasses from Accoutrement; tray from Morris Home & Garden Wares.
Above: Rug from Plumes Gifts; plates and canister are Christopher Vine Design.

HAZELNUT AND ADZUKI BEAN BALLS WITH PEPPER SALAD

1 cup (200g) adzuki beans
1 medium onion, grated
2 cloves garlic, crushed
1 tablespoon chopped fresh thyme
1 vegetable stock cube
½ cup (55g) packaged
   ground hazelnuts
¾ cup (50g) stale breadcrumbs
1 egg, lightly beaten
oil for deep-frying

PEPPER SALAD
1 bulb (about 70g) garlic
1 medium red pepper, sliced
1 medium green pepper, sliced
1 medium yellow pepper, sliced
¼ cup (60ml) olive oil

DRESSING
2 tablespoons hazelnut oil
⅓ cup (80ml) extra virgin olive oil
2 tablespoons dried currants
1 tablespoon honey
¼ cup (35g) roasted hazelnuts
1 tablespoon fresh thyme sprigs

Place beans in bowl, cover well with water, cover, stand overnight.

Drain beans, add to pan of boiling water, simmer, uncovered, about 30 minutes or until tender; drain. Blend or process beans with onion, garlic, thyme and crumbled stock cube until smooth; stir in nuts, breadcrumbs and egg. Shape 2 level teaspoons of mixture into balls, deep-fry in hot oil until browned; drain on absorbent paper. Serve over pepper salad; drizzle with dressing.

Pepper Salad: Separate garlic into cloves; do not peel. Combine garlic, peppers and oil in baking dish, bake in moderately hot oven about 45 minutes or until garlic and peppers are soft.

Dressing: Combine all ingredients in bowl; mix well.

Serves 4.

■ Beans best prepared a day ahead.
■ Storage: Covered, room temperature.
■ Freeze: Hazelnut and adzuki bean balls suitable.
■ Microwave: Not suitable.

◉ Add 150g sliced prosciutto or ham to pepper salad.

BEAN AND SPINACH CROSTINI

2 medium eggplants
coarse cooking salt
oil for deep-frying
1 medium onion, thinly sliced
plain flour

TOPPING
1 cup (200g) haricot beans
2 tablespoons olive oil
2 cloves garlic, sliced
2 medium tomatoes, peeled, sliced
⅓ cup (80ml) tomato paste
¼ cup (60ml) dry red wine
¼ cup (60ml) water
1 bunch (about 650g) English
   spinach, shredded

CROSTINI
2 small French bread sticks
50g butter

Cut eggplants into 1cm slices, sprinkle with salt, stand 30 minutes.

Rinse eggplant slices under cold water, drain on absorbent paper. Deep-fry eggplant slices in hot oil until lightly browned; drain on absorbent paper. Toss onion in flour, deep-fry in hot oil until lightly browned; drain on absorbent paper. Place eggplant slices on crostini, spoon over topping, sprinkle with onions.

Topping: Place beans in bowl, cover well with cold water, cover, stand overnight.

Drain beans, add to pan of boiling water, simmer, covered, until tender; drain. Heat oil in pan, add garlic, cook, stirring, until fragrant. Add tomatoes, paste, wine, water and beans, simmer, uncovered, about 20 minutes or until mixture is thickened; add spinach, stir until wilted.

Crostini: Cut bread diagonally into 2cm slices; you need 8 slices. Brush both sides with butter, place in single layer on oven tray, bake in moderate oven about 20 minutes, turning once, or until browned and crisp.

Serves 4.

■ Topping and crostini can be prepared 2 days ahead.
■ Storage: Topping, covered, in refrigerator. Crostini, airtight container.
■ Freeze: Not suitable.
■ Microwave: Not suitable.

◉ Place a slice of ham on each crostini underneath eggplant.

LEFT: From top: Hazelnut and Adzuki Bean Balls with Pepper Salad, Bean and Spinach Crostini.

China from Corso de Fiori.

SHEPHERD'S BEAN PIE

1 cup (200g) black-eyed beans
2 tablespoons vegetable oil
1 medium onion, chopped
2 cloves garlic, crushed
2 medium carrots, chopped
200g mushrooms, quartered
425g can tomatoes
1 cup (250ml) tomato puree
2 tablespoons chopped fresh basil
1 vegetable stock cube
2 teaspoons Worcestershire sauce
1 teaspoon sugar

TOPPING
5 large (about 1.25kg) potatoes,
    peeled, chopped
30g butter
2 tablespoons milk
1/3 cup (25g) grated parmesan cheese
1/3 cup (80ml) cream

Place beans in bowl, cover well with water, cover, stand overnight.

Drain beans, add to pan of boiling water, simmer, uncovered, about 20 minutes or until tender; drain. Blend or process half the beans until finely chopped, reserve remaining beans.

Heat oil in pan, add onion, garlic, carrots and mushrooms, cook, stirring, until onion is soft. Add undrained crushed tomatoes, puree, basil, crumbled stock cube, sauce and sugar. Simmer, uncovered, about 10 minutes or until vegetables are tender and mixture thickened slightly. Stir in pureed beans and reserved beans; mix well.

Spoon mixture into ovenproof dish (2.5 litre/10 cup capacity), spoon topping over mixture. Place dish on oven tray, bake in moderately hot oven about 20 minutes or until lightly browned and hot.

Topping: Boil, steam or microwave potatoes until soft; drain. Mash potatoes with butter, milk, cheese and cream, beat until smooth and creamy.

Serves 6.

■ Recipe can be made a day ahead.
■ Storage: Covered, in refrigerator.
■ Freeze: Not suitable.
■ Microwave: Topping suitable.

◉ Omit half the beans; replace with150g chopped chorizo sausage or salami in onion mixture.

CHICK PEA, SPINACH AND FETA CHEESE SALAD

2 x 310g cans chick peas,
    rinsed, drained
200g feta cheese, cubed
2 medium red peppers, thinly sliced
1 bunch (250g) rocket
1 radicchio lettuce
1/2 bunch (about 325g)
    English spinach

HERB CROUTONS
1/2 x 600g loaf herb bread
80g butter, melted

DRESSING
2/3 cup (160ml) olive oil
1 tablespoon balsamic vinegar
1/4 cup (60ml) white wine vinegar
1 clove garlic, crushed
1 1/2 teaspoons sambal oelek
1 teaspoon brown sugar

Combine chick peas, cheese, peppers, herb croutons and dressing in bowl; mix gently. Combine rocket, lettuce and spinach in another bowl, top with chick pea mixture.

Herb Croutons: Remove crusts from bread, cut bread into 2cm cubes. Toss bread with butter in bowl until bread is well coated. Place bread in single layer on oven tray, bake in moderate oven about 10 minutes or until crisp; cool.

Dressing: Combine all ingredients in jar; shake well.

Serves 4 to 6.

■ Dressing and croutons can be made a day ahead.
■ Storage: Dressing, covered, in refrigerator. Croutons, airtight container.
■ Freeze: Not suitable.
■ Microwave: Not suitable.

◉ Add 6 chopped, cooked bacon rashers to salad.

ABOVE: From left: Chick Pea, Spinach and Feta Cheese Salad, Shepherd's Bean Pie.

HARICOT BEAN LETTUCE CUPS

⅔ cup (130g) dried haricot beans
1 tablespoon vegetable oil
4 green shallots, chopped
1 clove garlic, crushed
227g can water chestnuts, drained, chopped
1 bunch (about 650g) bok choy, shredded
1 cup (80g) mung bean sprouts
4 lettuce leaves

SAUCE
1½ tablespoons light soy sauce
1 tablespoon hoi sin sauce
1 teaspoon sesame oil
2 teaspoons grated fresh ginger

Place beans in bowl, cover well with cold water, cover, stand overnight.

Drain beans, add to pan of boiling water, simmer, uncovered, about 30 minutes or until tender; drain.

Heat oil in pan, add shallots and garlic, cook, stirring, until shallots are soft. Add beans, water chestnuts, bok choy, sprouts and sauce, cook, stirring, until bok choy is wilted. Spoon bean mixture onto lettuce leaves to serve.

Sauce: Combine all ingredients in bowl; mix well.

Serves 4.

■ Beans best prepared a day ahead.
■ Storage: Covered, room temperature.
■ Freeze: Not suitable.
■ Microwave: Not suitable.

◉ Omit the beans; replace with 250g cooked, minced beef.

SPINACH AND SOYA BEAN LOAF

½ bunch (about 325g) English spinach
1½ tablespoons olive oil
1 large onion, chopped
2 cloves garlic, crushed
4 sticks celery, chopped
2 medium zucchini, chopped
2 medium tomatoes, peeled, chopped
2 tablespoons tomato paste
1 vegetable stock cube
445g can soya beans, rinsed, drained
½ cup (50g) packaged breadcrumbs
⅓ cup chopped fresh parsley
3 eggs, lightly beaten

VINAIGRETTE
⅓ cup (80ml) olive oil
¼ cup (60ml) lemon juice
1 teaspoon seeded mustard
½ teaspoon sugar
½ teaspoon seasoned pepper

Cut thick stalks from spinach, add leaves to pan of boiling water for 30 seconds; drain, rinse under cold water, drain well.

Line 11cm x 23cm ovenproof glass loaf dish with three-quarters of the spinach leaves, allowing leaves to overhang edges. Heat oil in pan, add onion, garlic, celery and zucchini, cook, stirring, until vegetables are soft. Add tomatoes, paste and crumbled stock cube, simmer, uncovered, 5 minutes. Remove from heat, stand 10 minutes. Add beans, breadcrumbs, parsley and eggs; mix well.

Spoon mixture into prepared dish, fold leaves over filling, top with remaining leaves. Cover dish loosely with foil, bake in moderate oven about 1 hour or until firm; cool. Cover dish, refrigerate several hours or overnight. Serve loaf sliced with vinaigrette.

Vinaigrette: Combine all ingredients in jar; shake well.

Serves 6.

■ Recipe best made a day ahead.
■ Storage: Covered, in refrigerator.
■ Freeze: Not suitable.
■ Microwave: Not suitable.

◉ Add 125g chopped ham to mixture with soya beans.

LIMA BEAN, EGG AND POTATO SALAD

1 cup (200g) baby lima beans
500g baby new potatoes, halved
150g snow peas
4 green shallots, chopped
200g button mushrooms, sliced
1 small green cucumber,
**   seeded, chopped**
1 medium red pepper, chopped
8 hard-boiled eggs, quartered
⅓ cup (15g) alfalfa sprouts

MAYONNAISE
1 egg
1 teaspoon French mustard
1 clove garlic, crushed
1 tablespoon lemon juice
1 cup (250ml) olive oil
1 tablespoon chopped fresh thyme
⅓ cup (80ml) milk, approximately

Place beans in bowl, cover well with cold water, cover, stand overnight.

Drain beans, add to pan of boiling water, simmer, uncovered, about 30 minutes or until tender; drain, rinse under cold water, drain well.

Boil, steam or microwave potatoes and snow peas separately until just tender; drain, rinse under cold water, drain well.

Combine beans, potatoes, snow peas, shallots, mushrooms, cucumber, pepper and eggs in bowl; drizzle with mayonnaise, top with sprouts.

Mayonnaise: Process egg, mustard, garlic and juice until combined. Gradually add oil in a thin stream while motor is operating; process until thick. Transfer mixture to bowl, stir in thyme, whisk in enough milk to give a thin mayonnaise.

Serves 4.

■ Beans best prepared a day ahead. Mayonnaise can be made 2 days ahead.
■ Storage: Beans, covered, room temperature. Mayonnaise, covered, in refrigerator.
■ Freeze: Not suitable.
■ Microwave: Potatoes and snow peas suitable.

◉ Omit eggs; replace with 400g chopped salami.

SOYA BEAN RING WITH TOMATO SALSA

10 cherry tomatoes, halved
1 tablespoon olive oil
2 medium onions, finely chopped
2 cloves garlic, crushed
1 bunch (about 650g) English
**   spinach, shredded**
1 small carrot, grated
1 small zucchini, grated
1 cup (200g) cottage cheese
445g can soya beans, rinsed, drained
½ cup (60g) pecans, chopped
⅓ cup (50g) dried currants
¼ cup (60ml) tomato paste
1 tablespoon chopped fresh dill
1 tablespoon chopped fresh oregano
1 tablespoon chopped fresh thyme
¼ cup (20g) grated parmesan cheese
1 cup (70g) stale breadcrumbs
2 eggs, lightly beaten

TOMATO SALSA
200g cherry tomatoes, halved
4 green shallots, chopped
2 tablespoons shredded fresh basil
1 tablespoon red wine vinegar
¼ cup (60ml) olive oil
1 clove garlic, crushed

Place tomatoes, cut side down, around base of greased ovenproof ring mould (2.5 litre/10 cup capacity). Heat oil in pan, add onions and garlic, cook, stirring, until onions are soft. Boil, steam or microwave spinach until just wilted; drain well, chop finely.

Combine onion mixture and spinach with remaining ingredients in bowl; mix well. Press firmly into mould.

Bake, uncovered, in moderate oven about 50 minutes or until firm. Stand 5 minutes before turning onto plate. Serve with tomato salsa.

Tomato Salsa: Combine all ingredients in bowl; mix well.

Serves 6.

■ Recipe can be made 3 hours ahead.
■ Storage: Covered, in refrigerator.
■ Freeze: Not suitable.
■ Microwave: Spinach suitable.

◉ Add 4 drained, chopped anchovies to tomato salsa.

LEFT: Clockwise from left: Lima Bean, Egg and Potato Salad, Spinach and Soya Bean Loaf, Haricot Bean Lettuce Cups.
ABOVE: Soya Bean Ring with Tomato Salsa.

Above: Plate is Christopher Vine Design.

89

BROAD BEAN AND SPICY CROUTON SALAD

1kg fresh broad beans
¼ cup (60ml) olive oil
2 large red Spanish onions, chopped
2 cloves garlic, crushed
1 teaspoon ground cumin
1 teaspoon ground coriander
½ cup (125ml) tomato juice
¼ cup (60ml) water
1 tablespoon sweet chilli sauce
250g cherry tomatoes
2½ cups (250g) mung bean sprouts
2 large avocados, chopped

SPICY CROUTONS
½ loaf white unsliced bread
½ cup (125ml) olive oil
1 clove garlic, crushed
1 teaspoon dried chilli flakes
½ teaspoon dried oregano leaves

Remove beans from pods. Add beans to pan of boiling water, simmer, uncovered, about 5 minutes or until tender; drain, rinse under cold water, drain. Remove skins from beans.

Heat oil in pan, add onions, garlic, cumin and coriander, cook, stirring, until onions are soft. Remove from heat, stir in juice, water and sauce; cool.

Combine beans, onion mixture and remaining ingredients in bowl; serve with spicy croutons.

Spicy Croutons: Cut bread into 1.5cm cubes. Combine cubes with remaining ingredients in bowl; mix well. Place cubes in single layer on oven tray, toast in moderately hot oven about 10 minutes.

Serves 4.

■ Croutons can be made a week ahead.
■ Storage: Airtight container.
■ Freeze: Croutons suitable.
■ Microwave: Not suitable.

◉ Add 200g chopped, cooked speck or 4 rashers bacon to salad.

SPICY CHICK PEA NAAN WITH PEACH CHUTNEY

2 teaspoons (7g) dried yeast
¼ teaspoon sugar
¼ cup (60ml) warm water
¾ cup (180ml) warm milk
1 egg, lightly beaten
¼ cup (60ml) plain yogurt
1 tablespoon honey
½ cup (125ml) vegetable oil
1 cup (150g) white plain flour
2 cups (320g) wholemeal plain flour
⅓ cup (50g) besan flour
1 teaspoon salt
2 teaspoons caraway seeds

FILLING
2 x 310g cans chick peas,
  rinsed, drained
⅓ cup (80ml) plain yogurt
1 teaspoon ground cumin
½ teaspoon ground cardamom
½ teaspoon chilli powder

PEACH CHUTNEY
1 tablespoon vegetable oil
1 large onion, chopped
1 teaspoon curry powder
1 teaspoon ground allspice
½ teaspoon black mustard seeds
2 x 425g cans peaches in syrup,
  drained, chopped
⅓ cup (65g) brown sugar
⅓ cup (80ml) brown vinegar
1 tablespoon chopped
  fresh coriander

Combine yeast, sugar and water in small bowl; stand in warm place about 10 minutes or until frothy. Combine milk, egg, yogurt, honey and 2 tablespoons of the oil in bowl.

Sift flours into large bowl, stir in salt, seeds, yeast mixture and milk mixture; mix to a soft dough. Knead dough on floured surface about 5 minutes or until smooth and elastic. Place dough in oiled bowl, stand, covered, in warm place about 1 hour or until doubled in size.

Divide dough into 8 portions. Roll each portion on floured surface to 15cm round. Divide filling between 4 rounds, leaving 1cm border around edges. Brush edges with water, top with remaining rounds, pinch edges together.

Heat a little of the remaining oil in pan, cook 1 round until lightly browned on both sides; place on oven tray. Repeat with remaining oil and rounds. Bake rounds, uncovered, in moderately hot oven about 10 minutes. Serve with peach chutney.

Filling: Process chick peas until finely minced, stir in remaining ingredients.

Peach Chutney: Heat oil in pan, add onion, spices and seeds, cook, stirring, until onion is soft. Stir in peaches, sugar and vinegar, simmer, uncovered, stirring occasionally, until mixture is thick; cool. Stir in coriander.

Serves 4.

- Chutney, without coriander, can be made a week ahead.
- Storage: Covered, in refrigerator.
- Freeze: Naan suitable.
- Microwave: Peach chutney suitable.

◉ Add ⅔ cup (130g) finely chopped, cooked chicken to filling.

CHILLI BEANS WITH PUMPKIN CORNBREAD

You will need about 400g peeled, seeded pumpkin for this recipe.

1 tablespoon vegetable oil
1 medium onion, chopped
2 cloves garlic, crushed
2 teaspoons ground cumin
2 teaspoons paprika
½ teaspoon sambal oelek
2 teaspoons chopped fresh oregano
2 medium carrots, sliced
2 x 425g cans tomatoes
1 teaspoon vegetable stock powder
½ cup (125ml) water
2 x 310g cans 4 bean mix,
  rinsed, drained
½ medium red pepper, chopped
1 medium green pepper, chopped

PUMPKIN CORNBREAD
1¾ cups (260g) cornmeal
¾ cup (110g) self-raising flour
½ teaspoon bicarbonate of soda
1 cup (250ml) buttermilk
1 cup cold cooked mashed pumpkin
1 egg, lightly beaten
60g butter, melted
¼ cup (60ml) maple-flavoured syrup
¼ teaspoon ground cardamom

Heat oil in pan, add onion and garlic, cook, stirring, until onion is soft. Stir in cumin, paprika, sambal oelek and oregano, cook, stirring, 2 minutes. Add carrots, undrained crushed tomatoes, stock powder and water, simmer, covered, 30 minutes. Add beans and peppers, simmer, uncovered, 15 minutes. Serve chilli beans with pumpkin cornbread.

Pumpkin Cornbread: Grease 23cm square slab cake pan, cover base with baking paper. Combine all ingredients in bowl; mix well. Pour into prepared pan. Bake in moderate oven about 25 minutes or until lightly browned and cooked through.

Serves 4 to 6.

- Chilli beans can be made a day ahead.
- Storage: Covered, in refrigerator.
- Freeze: Suitable.
- Microwave: Chilli beans suitable.

◉ Substitute 300g cooked, minced beef for 1 can 4 bean mix. Add to chilli bean mixture with remaining beans.

FAR LEFT: From left: Broad Bean and Spicy Crouton Salad, Spicy Chick Pea Naan with Peach Chutney.
LEFT: Chilli Beans with Pumpkin Cornbread.

Far left: Wooden bowl and platter from Corso de Fiori. Left: Bowl from Accoutrement; spoon from Country Furniture Antiques.

CURRIED LENTIL PARCELS WITH HERB SAUCE

½ cup (100g) white rice
500g fresh broad beans
¾ cup (150g) brown lentils
¼ cup (60ml) vegetable oil
1 large onion, chopped
1 tablespoon curry powder
3 teaspoons seeded mustard
2 tablespoons chopped
    fresh coriander
2 tablespoons chopped unsalted
    roasted cashews
2 tablespoons sour cream
16 sheets fillo pastry
125g butter, melted
1 tablespoon sesame seeds

HERB SAUCE
1 cup (250ml) sour cream
1 tablespoon chopped fresh chives
1 tablespoon chopped
    fresh coriander
1½ tablespoons lemon juice

Add rice to pan of boiling water, boil, uncovered, until tender; drain. Remove beans from pods, add beans to pan of boiling water, simmer, uncovered, 2 minutes; drain, rinse under cold water, drain. Remove skins from beans.

Add lentils to pan of boiling water, boil, uncovered, about 15 minutes or until tender; drain. Heat oil in pan, add onion, cook, stirring, until soft. Add curry powder and mustard, cook, stirring, until fragrant; cool. Combine rice, beans, lentils, onion mixture, coriander, nuts and cream in bowl; mix well.

Layer 2 pastry sheets together, brushing each with butter. Fold layered pastry in half lengthways to form a long strip, brush with more butter. Place ½ cup (125ml) of lentil mixture at 1 end of pastry strip. Fold end over to form a triangle, continue folding until end of pastry, brush with more butter; sprinkle with sesame seeds.

Place on greased oven tray. Repeat with remaining pastry sheets, butter and filling. Bake, uncovered, in moderately hot oven about 15 minutes or until browned and crisp. Serve with herb sauce.

Herb Sauce: Combine all ingredients in bowl; mix well.

Makes 8.

■ Curried lentil parcels can be made a
   day ahead.
■ Storage: Covered, in refrigerator.
■ Freeze: Uncooked parcels suitable.
■ Microwave: Rice and beans suitable.

◉ Omit rice; replace with 500g
   cooked chicken mince in filling.

LEFT: From back: Broad Bean, Chick Pea and Garlic Salad, Curried Lentil Parcels with Herb Sauce.
RIGHT: Bean and Kumara Nachos.

Left: Pewter servers, bowl, plate and garlic tile from Corso de Fiori. Right: China from Accoutrement; cane shelf from Corso de Fiori.

BROAD BEAN, CHICK PEA AND GARLIC SALAD

¾ cup (150g) dried chick peas
180g green beans
10 baby potatoes, halved
2 medium carrots, chopped
1¼ cups (185g) frozen broad
    beans, thawed
½ teaspoon seasoned pepper

GARLIC DRESSING
½ cup (125ml) plain yogurt
2 cloves garlic, crushed
1 egg yolk
⅔ cup (160ml) olive oil
2 tablespoons lemon juice

Place chick peas in bowl, cover well with water, cover, stand overnight.

Drain chick peas, add to large pan of boiling water, boil, uncovered, about 30 minutes or until tender; drain.

Cut green beans into 3cm lengths. Boil, steam or microwave green beans, potatoes and carrots separately until tender; drain, rinse under cold water, drain.

Add broad beans to pan of boiling water, boil, uncovered, 3 minutes; drain. Remove skins. Combine chick peas, vegetables, broad beans and pepper in bowl; drizzle with dressing.

Garlic Dressing: Blend or process all ingredients until smooth.

Serves 4.

■ Recipe can be prepared a day ahead.
■ Storage: Covered, in refrigerator.
■ Freeze: Not suitable.
■ Microwave: Beans, potatoes and
   carrots suitable.

◉ Cut 200g squid hoods into rings,
   stir-fry squid in a little oil, serve
over salad.

BEAN AND KUMARA NACHOS

650g kumara, chopped
2 tablespoons olive oil
2 teaspoons cumin seeds
2 teaspoons coriander seeds
1 medium onion, sliced
2 cloves garlic, crushed
1 small fresh red chilli, chopped
1 teaspoon paprika
410g can tomatoes
½ medium red pepper, chopped
½ medium green pepper, chopped
310g can red kidney beans,
    rinsed, drained
200g packet corn chips
2 cups (250g) grated tasty cheese
1 medium avocado, sliced
½ cup (125ml) sour cream
2 tablespoons chopped
    fresh coriander

Combine kumara, 1 tablespoon of the oil and seeds in baking dish, bake, uncovered, in moderate oven about 30 minutes or until tender. Heat remaining oil in pan, add onion, garlic, chilli and paprika, cook until onion is soft. Add undrained crushed tomatoes and peppers, simmer, covered, 5 minutes; stir in beans. Divide corn chips between 4 ovenproof dishes (1¾ cup/430ml capacity). Top with bean mixture, then kumara, sprinkle with cheese. Bake, uncovered, in moderate oven about 10 minutes or until hot. Serve with avocado, cream and coriander.

Serves 4.

■ Kumara and bean mixture can be
   prepared a day ahead.
■ Storage: Covered, in refrigerator.
■ Freeze: Not suitable.
■ Microwave: Bean mixture suitable.

◉ Add 1 cup (150g) chopped, cooked
   chicken to bean mixture.

SPLIT PEA BURGERS WITH TOMATO SALAD

1 cup (200g) yellow split peas
3 cups (750ml) water
1 vegetable stock cube
¼ cup (25g) packaged breadcrumbs
1 medium old potato, grated
1 medium carrot, grated
¼ cup (35g) sesame seeds, toasted
1 egg, lightly beaten
2 teaspoons curry powder

TOMATO SALAD
4 egg tomatoes
4 green shallots, chopped
2 tablespoons shredded fresh mint
¼ cup (60ml) olive oil
3 teaspoons black bean sauce
2 tablespoons lime juice

Combine peas, water and crumbled stock cube in pan, simmer, covered, about 20 minutes or until peas are very soft and water is absorbed. You will need 2 cups (500ml) pea mixture.

Combine pea mixture with remaining ingredients in bowl. Divide mixture into 12 patties. Cook patties in oiled pan, or on well-greased barbecue plate or grill until browned.
Tomato Salad: Cut tomatoes into wedges, combine with remaining ingredients in bowl, cover, refrigerate 1 hour.

Serves 4.

■ Uncooked burgers can be made a day ahead. Tomato salad can be made 3 hours ahead.
■ Storage: Covered, separately, in refrigerator.
■ Freeze: Not suitable.
■ Microwave: Split peas suitable.

◎ Add 60g sliced lamb prosciutto or salami to tomato salad.

BLACK-EYED BEANS WITH PASTA AND TOMATO PESTO

¾ cup (150g) black-eyed beans
125g bow tie pasta
2 tablespoons olive oil
4 medium zucchini, chopped
1 medium red Spanish onion, chopped
200g button mushrooms, halved
310g can butter beans, rinsed, drained
⅓ cup (25g) parmesan cheese flakes

TOMATO PESTO
½ cup (80g) pine nuts
2 cups fresh basil leaves, firmly packed
3 cloves garlic, crushed
1 medium tomato, chopped
¾ cup (60g) grated parmesan cheese
½ cup (125ml) extra virgin olive oil

Add black-eyed beans to pan of boiling water, simmer, uncovered, about 20 minutes or until beans are just tender; drain, rinse, drain. Add pasta to pan of boiling water, boil, uncovered, until just tender; drain, rinse, drain. Heat oil in pan, add zucchini, onion and mushrooms, cook, stirring, until vegetables are just tender. Stir in black-eyed beans, pasta and butter beans; mix well. Serve salad warm; drizzle with tomato pesto, top with cheese.
Tomato Pesto: Blend or process nuts, basil, garlic, tomato and cheese until smooth. Gradually add oil in thin stream while motor is operating, process until thick.

Serves 4 to 6.

■ Recipe best made close to serving.
■ Freeze: Not suitable.
■ Microwave: Pasta suitable.

◎ Add 300g chopped salami or ham to salad.

ABOVE: From left: Split Pea Burgers with Tomato Salad, Black-Eyed Beans with Pasta and Tomato Pesto.
RIGHT: Chick Pea Patties with Spicy Onions.

Above: Slotted spoon from Country Furniture Antiques. Right: Plate from Lifestyle Imports.

CHICK PEA PATTIES WITH SPICY ONIONS

60g butter
1 cup (150g) plain flour
2/3 cup (160ml) milk
2 eggs, lightly beaten
2 small zucchini, grated
2 x 310g cans chick peas, rinsed,
    drained, mashed
2 cups (140g) stale breadcrumbs
plain flour
oil for shallow-frying

YOGURT SAUCE
1 cup (250ml) plain yogurt
2 tablespoons fruit chutney
2 teaspoons grated lime rind
1 tablespoon chopped
    fresh coriander
1 tablespoon chopped fresh mint

SPICY ONIONS
2 tablespoons vegetable oil
2 teaspoons ground cumin
2 teaspoons ground coriander
4 medium onions, sliced

Melt butter in pan, stir in flour, stir over heat until mixture is dry and grainy. Remove from heat, gradually stir in milk, stir over heat until mixture forms a ball in pan. Remove from heat, stir in eggs, zucchini, chick peas and breadcrumbs.

Drop 1/4 cups (60ml) of mixture into flour; using floured hands, shape into patties. Shallow-fry patties in hot oil until lightly browned on both sides; drain on absorbent paper. Serve with yogurt sauce and spicy onions.

Yogurt Sauce: Combine all ingredients in bowl; mix well.

Spicy Onions: Heat oil in pan, add spices, cook, stirring, until fragrant, add onions, cook, stirring, until onions are soft and browned.

Makes about 15.

■ Recipe can be made a day ahead.
■ Storage: Covered, in refrigerator.
■ Freeze: Not suitable.
■ Microwave: Not suitable.

● Substitute 3/4 cup (110g) cooked, chopped lamb for zucchini in patties.

SOUR CREAM, BEAN AND MUSHROOM CASSEROLE

¾ cup (150g) dried lima beans
60g butter
1 tablespoon olive oil
2 cloves garlic, crushed
700g button mushrooms, quartered
½ cup (125ml) dry white wine
2 x 310g cans kidney beans,
   rinsed, drained
1 cup (250ml) sour cream
1 tablespoon chopped fresh oregano
2 teaspoons chopped fresh thyme
1 tablespoon chopped fresh parsley
2 teaspoons seeded mustard
2 teaspoons grated lemon rind

Place lima beans in bowl, cover well with water, cover, stand overnight.

Drain lima beans, remove skins, add beans to pan of boiling water, simmer, covered, about 40 minutes or until tender; drain.

Heat half of the butter and oil in pan, add garlic and three-quarters of the mushrooms, cook, stirring, until mushrooms are soft. Add wine, simmer, uncovered, 5 minutes, add lima beans, kidney beans, cream, herbs, mustard and rind, cook, stirring, until sauce is heated through.

Heat remaining butter in another pan, add remaining mushrooms, cook over high heat until mushrooms are lightly browned. Serve over casserole.

Serves 4.

■ Lima beans best prepared a
   day ahead.
■ Storage: Covered, room temperature.
■ Freeze: Not suitable.
■ Microwave: Not suitable.

◉ Omit 1 can kidney beans, replace
   with 400g sliced veal schnitzel;
add veal to pan with extra mushrooms, cook, stirring, until tender.

LETTUCE ROLLS WITH SWEET AND SOUR SAUCE

1 cup (200g) yellow split peas
1 tablespoon vegetable oil
6 green shallots, chopped
2 cloves garlic, crushed
2 teaspoons grated fresh ginger
2 sticks celery, finely chopped
1 medium carrot, grated
1 medium red pepper, finely chopped
¼ teaspoon five-spice powder
1 tablespoon hoi sin sauce
2 tablespoons light soy sauce
1 teaspoon sesame oil
2 teaspoons cornflour
½ cup (125ml) vegetable stock
2 iceberg lettuce

SWEET AND SOUR SAUCE
2 teaspoons cornflour
¾ cup (180ml) sweetened
   pineapple juice
2 tablespoons white vinegar
2 tablespoons tomato sauce
2 teaspoons sugar

Add peas to pan of boiling water, simmer, uncovered, about 30 minutes or until tender; drain. Heat oil in pan, add shallots, garlic, ginger, celery, carrot, pepper and five-spice powder, cook, stirring, until vegetables are soft. Stir in sauces, sesame oil and blended cornflour and vegetable stock. Stir until mixture boils and thickens, simmer 1 minute; stir in peas.

Drop lettuce leaves into pan of boiling water, drain immediately, add to bowl of iced water; drain, pat dry with absorbent paper. Remove hard centre from leaves, place 2 level tablespoons of mixture onto base of each leaf, roll once, fold in sides, roll up to form parcels. Steam rolls in steamer over wok or large pan about 15 minutes or until hot. Serve with sweet and sour sauce.

Sweet and Sour Sauce: Combine blended cornflour and juice with remaining ingredients in pan, stir over heat until mixture boils and thickens.

Serves 6.

■ Filling and sauce can be made a
   day ahead.
■ Storage: Covered, separately,
   in refrigerator.
■ Freeze: Not suitable.
■ Microwave: Completed rolls and
   sauce suitable.

◉ Omit half the split peas; cook
   200g minced beef in pan before
adding vegetables.

LEFT: From left: Lettuce Rolls with Sweet and Sour Sauce, Sour Cream, Bean and Mushroom Casserole.

China from Portmeirion; basket and tea-towel from Home & Garden on the Mall.

SPAGHETTI WITH LENTILS AND CORN

½ cup (100g) red lentils
2 cobs fresh corn
⅓ cup (80ml) olive oil
4 cloves garlic, sliced
1 medium red Spanish onion, sliced
1 medium red pepper, sliced
2 tablespoons chopped fresh oregano
1 tablespoon chopped fresh thyme
500g spaghetti pasta

HERB DRESSING
1 tablespoon red wine vinegar
1 clove garlic, crushed
¼ cup (60ml) extra virgin olive oil
1 tablespoon chopped fresh oregano
2 teaspoons chopped fresh thyme

Add lentils to pan of boiling water, boil, uncovered, about 8 minutes or until tender, drain. Boil, steam or microwave corn until tender; drain, rinse under cold water, drain. Cut kernels from cobs.

Heat oil in pan, add garlic, onion, pepper and herbs, cook, stirring, until heated through; stir in lentils and corn. Add pasta to large pan of boiling water, boil, uncovered, until just tender; drain. Combine pasta and lentil mixture in bowl; drizzle with herb dressing.

Herb Dressing: Combine all ingredients in jar; shake well.

Serves 4.

■ Recipe best made just before serving.
■ Freeze: Not suitable.
■ Microwave: Pasta and corn suitable.

◉ Add 185g can drained, flaked tuna to lentil mixture before adding pasta.

TOMATOES WITH LIMA BEANS AND CHEESY CROUTES

1 cup (200g) dried lima beans
6 medium tomatoes, peeled
1 tablespoon chopped fresh mint
2 tablespoons chopped fresh chives
¼ cup (40g) pine nuts, toasted
50g butter
300g button mushrooms, quartered

DRESSING
1 egg yolk
2 tablespoons cider vinegar
1 clove garlic, crushed
¼ teaspoon sugar
¾ cup (180ml) extra virgin olive oil

CHEESY CROUTES
6 slices white bread
40g butter, melted
¼ cup (20g) grated parmesan cheese

Place beans in bowl, cover well with water, cover, stand overnight.

Drain beans, place in pan, cover with water, simmer, covered, about 40 minutes or until tender; drain, cool.

Cut tops from tomatoes, scoop out seeds, discard seeds and tops. Combine beans, herbs, nuts and half the dressing in bowl. Spoon mixture into tomatoes, refrigerate 1 hour.

Heat butter in pan, add mushrooms, cover, cook until tender. Place tomatoes on croutes, top with remaining dressing, serve with mushrooms.

Dressing: Combine egg yolk, vinegar, garlic and sugar in bowl, gradually whisk in oil in a thin steady stream.

Cheesy Croutes: Cut 8cm rounds from bread. Brush both sides of bread with butter, sprinkle with cheese. Place on oven tray, bake in moderate oven about 20 minutes until well browned and crisp.

Serves 6.

■ Beans best prepared a day ahead. Croutes can be made a day ahead.
■ Storage: Beans, covered, room temperature. Croutes, airtight container.
■ Freeze: Not suitable.
■ Microwave: Not suitable.

◉ Add 3 chopped, cooked bacon rashers to lima bean mixture.

WARM LENTIL SALAD WITH GOATS' CHEESE

1.5 litres (6 cups) water
1 vegetable stock cube
1½ cups (300g) brown lentils
½ cup (125ml) olive oil
2 cloves garlic, crushed
300g baby onions, quartered
¼ cup (60ml) brown vinegar
½ cup (125ml) dry white wine
¼ cup (50g) brown sugar
250g cherry tomatoes
¼ cup firmly packed fresh flat-leafed parsley leaves
1 tablespoon chopped fresh oregano
½ cup (75g) dried currants
¼ cup (40g) pine nuts, toasted
8 large English spinach leaves
200g goats' cheese, chopped

Add water and crumbled stock cube to pan, bring to boil, add lentils, simmer, uncovered, about 15 minutes or until tender; drain.

Heat half the oil in pan, add garlic and onions, cook, stirring, 1 minute. Stir in vinegar, wine and sugar, simmer, uncovered, over low heat, stirring occasionally, about 15 minutes or until onions are caramelised and liquid evaporated. Stir in remaining oil, lentils, tomatoes, herbs, currants and nuts, stir until heated through. Add torn spinach leaves and cheese, stir until cheese is starting to melt.

Serves 4.

■ Recipe best made just before serving.
■ Freeze: Not suitable.
■ Microwave: Not suitable.

◉ Add 200g chopped ham to salad with spinach and cheese.

FELAFEL PITTA POCKETS

¾ cup (135g) dried broad beans
¾ cup (150g) dried chick peas
1 small onion, chopped
2 cloves garlic, crushed
2 teaspoons ground cumin
pinch cayenne pepper
2 tablespoons chopped fresh coriander
oil for deep-frying
3 medium tomatoes, peeled, seeded, chopped
2 small green cucumbers, seeded, chopped
1 medium red Spanish onion, chopped
½ cup chopped fresh mint
½ cup chopped fresh parsley
2 tablespoons olive oil
1 tablespoon lemon juice
4 round wholemeal pitta pocket breads
5 iceberg lettuce leaves, shredded
8 English spinach leaves, shredded

YOGURT SAUCE
1 cup (250ml) plain yogurt
¼ cup (60ml) tahini
⅓ cup (80ml) orange juice
¼ cup chopped fresh coriander
2 tablespoons sesame seeds, toasted

Cover beans well with water, cover, stand 48 hours; change water once. Cover chick peas well with water, cover, stand 15 hours.

Drain beans, peel and discard skins. Drain peas. Process beans, peas, small onion and garlic until finely minced. Transfer mixture to bowl, stir in cumin, pepper and coriander. Roll 2 level tablespoons of mixture into balls, stand 30 minutes. Deep-fry felafel in hot oil until browned and cooked; drain on absorbent paper.

Combine tomatoes, cucumbers, Spanish onion, herbs, oil and juice in bowl; mix well.

Cut pitta breads in half, split each half to form a pocket. Spread some of the yogurt sauce inside pockets, fill with some of the lettuce, spinach and tomato mixture. Top with felafel and remaining yogurt sauce.
Yogurt Sauce: Combine all ingredients in bowl; mix well.

Serves 4 to 6.

■ Felafel can be prepared a day ahead.
■ Storage: Covered, in refrigerator.
■ Freeze: Not suitable.
■ Microwave: Not suitable.

◉ Replace felafel with 300g sliced, cooked lamb.

FAR LEFT: From left: Spaghetti with Lentils and Corn, Tomatoes with Lima Beans and Cheesy Croutes.
LEFT: From left: Warm Lentil Salad with Goats' Cheese, Felafel Pitta Pockets.

Far left: Plates from Lifestyle Imports. Left: China from Lifestyle Imports; basket and glasses from Home & Garden on the Mall.

Vegetables

In a triumph of tastes and textures, we have used a fabulous range of vegetables for recipes with an international touch. They are innovative without being difficult, giving you new ways with favourites, plus the chance to try something you might not have thought of using, such as celeriac and okra. Vegetables are fantastic to work with because they are easy to handle, and mix and match brilliantly with all kinds of tantalising ingredients. You'll also enjoy tasty accompaniments, including our foccacia bread with fresh rosemary, corncakes, crisp olive croutes and more. The symbol 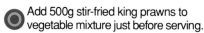 *indicates a variation, if desired.*

WARM VEGETABLE SALAD WITH MACADAMIAS

150g green beans
2 tablespoons olive oil
250g broccoli, chopped
150g sugar snap peas
150g snow peas
250g cherry tomatoes
60g snow pea sprouts
4 green shallots, chopped
1 cup (150g) roasted
   macadamias, chopped

DRESSING
⅓ cup (80ml) extra virgin olive oil
¼ cup (60ml) red wine vinegar
1 tablespoon chopped fresh thyme
1 teaspoon sugar
1 teaspoon cracked black peppercorns

Cut beans into 5cm lengths. Heat oil in wok or frying pan, add beans, broccoli and peas, stir-fry until well coated with oil. Add tomatoes, sprouts, shallots, half the nuts and dressing, stir-fry until just heated through. Serve sprinkled with remaining nuts.
Dressing: Combine all ingredients in jar; shake well.

Serves 4.

■ Recipe best made just before serving.
■ Freeze: Not suitable.
■ Microwave: Not suitable.

◉ Add 500g stir-fried king prawns to vegetable mixture just before serving.

ARTICHOKES WITH CREAMY MUSHROOM SAUCE

4 fresh medium globe artichokes
⅓ cup (80ml) lemon juice

CREAMY MUSHROOM SAUCE
40g butter
1 tablespoon olive oil
2 cloves garlic, crushed
250g button mushrooms, sliced
¼ cup (60ml) dry white wine
2 teaspoons seeded mustard
¼ cup (60ml) cream
½ cup (125ml) sour cream
1½ tablespoons chopped
   fresh oregano
1½ tablespoons chopped
   fresh chives
¼ cup (25g) drained sun-dried
   tomatoes, chopped

Trim stems from artichokes, remove tough outer leaves, trim tips of remaining leaves with scissors. Add artichokes and juice to large pan of boiling water, simmer, covered, about 30 minutes or until artichokes are tender; drain. Cut artichokes in half lengthways, remove hairy choke with spoon. Serve artichokes topped with creamy mushroom sauce.
Creamy Mushroom Sauce: Heat butter and oil in pan, add garlic and mushrooms, cook, stirring, until mushrooms are soft. Add wine, cook, uncovered, 2 minutes. Add mustard, creams, herbs and tomatoes, simmer, uncovered, about 3 minutes or until sauce thickens slightly.

Serves 4.

■ Sauce can be made 3 hours ahead.
■ Storage: Covered, in refrigerator.
■ Freeze: Not suitable.
■ Microwave: Sauce suitable.

◉ Add 3 chopped, cooked bacon rashers to sauce.

RIGHT: From left: Warm Vegetable Salad with Macadamias, Artichokes with Creamy Mushroom Sauce.

EASY VEGETABLE CURRY

30g ghee
2 medium tomatoes, peeled, chopped
1 cup (250ml) coconut cream
2 tablespoons plain yogurt
1 medium carrot, chopped
100g green beans, sliced
150g cauliflower, chopped
150g broccoli, chopped
150g button mushrooms, sliced

CURRY PASTE
1 medium onion, chopped
3 cloves garlic, crushed
2 teaspoons coriander seeds
2 teaspoons grated fresh ginger
1 teaspoon cumin seeds
1 teaspoon black mustard seeds
1 teaspoon sambal oelek
1 cinnamon stick
1½ tablespoons water
¼ teaspoon cardamom seeds
2 cloves
1 tablespoon tomato paste

Heat ghee in large pan, add curry paste, stir over medium heat 2 minutes. Stir in tomatoes, coconut cream and yogurt, simmer, covered, 10 minutes. Add carrot and beans, stir over heat 3 minutes. Add cauliflower, broccoli and mushrooms, stir over heat about 4 minutes or until vegetables are just tender.
Curry Paste: Blend or process all ingredients until smooth.
Serves 4.

■ Recipe can be made 3 hours ahead.
■ Storage: Covered, in refrigerator.
■ Freeze: Not suitable.
■ Microwave: Not suitable.

● Substitute 250g sliced, cooked chicken for mushrooms.

VEGETABLE PATTIES WITH CREAMY CHILLI SAUCE

3 large (about 600g) potatoes
1 medium onion, grated
1 medium carrot, grated
2 medium zucchini, grated
1 stick celery, grated
1 vegetable stock cube
1 tablespoon chopped fresh oregano
⅓ cup (25g) grated parmesan cheese
1 egg
¾ cup (110g) polenta
oil for shallow-frying

CREAMY CHILLI SAUCE
1 cup (250ml) cream
¼ teaspoon dried chilli flakes
⅓ cup (80ml) dry white wine
1 tablespoon shredded fresh basil

Boil, steam or microwave potatoes until tender; drain, mash, cool. Combine potatoes with vegetables, crumbled stock cube, oregano, cheese and egg in bowl; mix well. Divide mixture into 8 patties.

Toss patties in polenta, cover, refrigerate 30 minutes. Shallow-fry patties in hot oil until lightly browned on both sides. Place patties in single layer on oven tray, bake in moderate oven about 20 minutes or until cooked through. Serve patties with creamy chilli sauce.
Creamy Chilli Sauce: Combine cream, chilli flakes and wine in pan, simmer, uncovered, until slightly thickened; stir in basil.
Serves 4.

■ Patties can be made a day ahead.
■ Storage: Covered, in refrigerator.
■ Freeze: Patties suitable.
■ Microwave: Potatoes and creamy chilli sauce suitable.

● Add 210g can drained salmon to potato mixture.

BRAISED WITLOF WITH FIGS

60g butter
4 medium witlof, halved
1 clove garlic, sliced
3 sprigs fresh thyme
2 bay leaves
3 black peppercorns
3 teaspoons plain flour
1 cup (250ml) dry white wine
¼ cup (60ml) vegetable stock
1½ teaspoons sugar
2 tablespoons cream
1 large red coral lettuce
4 fresh figs, quartered
160g piece cheddar cheese, sliced

Heat butter in large heavy-based pan, add witlof, turn until coated in butter. Add garlic, thyme, bay leaves, peppercorns and flour, gently cook witlof, turning occasionally, until lightly browned. Stir in wine and stock, simmer, covered, until witlof is tender. Remove witlof from pan, stir in sugar and cream, stir over heat until hot. Strain sauce, discard thyme, bay leaves and peppercorns. Drizzle with sauce, serve with torn lettuce leaves, figs and cheese.

Serves 4 as an entree.

■ Recipe best made on day of serving.
■ Storage: Covered, in refrigerator.
■ Freeze: Not suitable.
■ Microwave: Not suitable.

◉ Serve salad with 60g sliced ham or prosciutto.

CAULIFLOWER CUPS WITH RED PEPPER SAUCE

8 sheets fillo pastry
60g butter

FILLING
500g cauliflower
30g butter
1 medium red Spanish onion,
   thinly sliced
⅓ cup (80ml) vegetable stock
½ bunch (about 325g)
   English spinach

RED PEPPER SAUCE
3 medium red peppers
1 clove garlic, crushed
2 tablespoons white vinegar
1 tablespoon olive oil

Grease 4 x 11cm pie tins. Layer 2 sheets of pastry together, brushing each with some of the butter. Cut pastry in half, cut each half into 4 pieces. Layer 4 pieces together, overlapping unevenly. Repeat with remaining pastry and butter. Press into prepared tins. Bake in moderate oven about 15 minutes or until well browned; cool pastry in tins. Spoon filling evenly into pastry cups, serve with red pepper sauce.
Filling: Cut cauliflower into flowerets. Heat butter in pan, add onion, cook, stirring, until soft. Add cauliflower and stock, simmer, covered, about 4 minutes or until cauliflower is just tender. Add spinach, stir until just wilted.

Red Pepper Sauce: Quarter peppers, remove seeds and membranes. Grill peppers, skin side up, until skin blisters and blackens. Peel away skin. Blend or process peppers, garlic, vinegar and oil until smooth. Place sauce in small pan, stir over heat until hot.

Serves 4.

■ Red pepper sauce and filling can be made a day ahead.
■ Storage: Covered, separately, in refrigerator.
■ Freeze: Not suitable.
■ Microwave: Filling suitable.

◉ Stir-fry 16 uncooked, peeled king prawns; serve with cauliflower cups.

LEFT: From back: Vegetable Patties with Creamy Chilli Sauce, Easy Vegetable Curry. ABOVE: From left: Braised Witlof with Figs, Cauliflower Cups with Red Pepper Sauce.

Left: China from Corso de Fiori. Above: Large plate from Powder Blue.

PAPRIKA CRUMBED PUMPKIN WITH RICOTTA TOPPING

500g pumpkin, peeled
plain flour
1 egg, lightly beaten
1 tablespoon milk
1 teaspoon celery salt
1 teaspoon paprika
1 tablespoon chopped fresh parsley
1 cup (70g) stale white breadcrumbs
oil for shallow-frying
2 tablespoons pine nuts, toasted

RICOTTA TOPPING
1 tablespoon olive oil
1 medium onion, grated
1 clove garlic, crushed
2 tablespoons chopped fresh basil
2 tablespoons chopped fresh chives
1½ cups (300g) ricotta cheese

Cut pumpkin into 8 thin slices. Toss pumpkin in flour, shake away excess flour, dip in combined egg and milk, then combined celery salt, paprika, parsley and breadcrumbs, refrigerate 30 minutes.

Shallow-fry pumpkin in hot oil on both sides until golden brown; drain on absorbent paper. Place pumpkin in single layer on oven tray, spoon over ricotta topping. Bake in moderate oven about 5 minutes or until just warm. Sprinkle with nuts.

Ricotta Topping: Heat oil in pan, add onion and garlic, cook, stirring, until onion is soft. Remove from heat, stir in herbs and cheese.

Serves 4.

■ Recipe can be prepared a day ahead.
■ Storage: Covered, in refrigerator.
■ Freeze: Not suitable.
■ Microwave: Not suitable.

◉ Thinly shred 2 smoked chicken breasts. Place chicken on crumbed pumpkin slices before ricotta topping.

SAUCY VEGETABLES WITH PARSLEY THYME DUMPLINGS

20g butter
1 large onion, chopped
1 clove garlic, crushed
400g baby new potatoes, halved
2 tablespoons plain flour
2 medium carrots, chopped
425g can tomatoes
2 tablespoons tomato paste
2 teaspoons chopped fresh thyme
2 cups (500ml) vegetable stock
4 medium zucchini, chopped
½ cup (125ml) cream

DUMPLINGS
1¼ cups (190g) self-raising flour
20g butter
1 tablespoon chopped fresh parsley
1 teaspoon chopped fresh thyme
½ cup (125ml) milk

Heat butter in large pan, add onion, garlic and potatoes, cook, stirring, until onion is soft. Stir in flour, cook, stirring, until well

combined. Add carrots, undrained crushed tomatoes, paste, thyme and stock, stir over heat until mixture boils; simmer, uncovered, about 20 minutes or until vegetables are tender. Stir in zucchini and cream.

Drop rounded teaspoons of dumpling mixture onto vegetable mixture. Simmer, uncovered, without stirring, about 15 minutes or until dumplings are cooked and zucchini tender. Turn dumplings over half way through cooking.

Dumplings: Sift flour into bowl, rub in butter. Stir in herbs and milk; mix until just combined.

Serves 4.

- ■ Recipe, without dumplings, can be made a day ahead.
- ■ Storage: Covered, in refrigerator.
- ■ Freeze: Not suitable.
- ■ Microwave: Not suitable.

◎ Add 250g sliced chicken fillets to pan with onion and garlic.

RATATOUILLE WITH CORNCAKES

2 tablespoons olive oil
1 medium onion, chopped
1 clove garlic, crushed
3 baby eggplants, sliced
2 medium zucchini, sliced
1 medium red pepper, chopped
1 medium green pepper, chopped
150g button mushrooms, halved
2 x 410g cans tomatoes
2 fresh medium tomatoes, chopped
⅓ cup shredded fresh basil
⅓ cup (25g) parmesan cheese flakes

CORNCAKES
⅔ cup (100g) wholemeal plain flour
½ cup (75g) white plain flour
130g can corn kernels, drained
2 x 130g cans creamed corn
2 eggs
¾ cup (180ml) milk

Heat oil in pan, add onion and garlic, cook, stirring, until onion is soft. Add eggplants, zucchini, peppers and mushrooms, cook, stirring occasionally, until vegetables are just tender; add undrained crushed tomatoes and chopped fresh tomatoes. Bring to boil, simmer, uncovered, about 20 minutes or until vegetables are soft and sauce is slightly thickened. Serve ratatouille with corncakes, top with basil and cheese.

Corncakes: Sift flours into bowl, add combined corn, creamed corn, eggs and milk, whisk until combined; stand 30 minutes. Pour ¼ cup (60ml) mixture into heated greased pan. Cook until bubbles appear on surface and underneath is browned, turn, brown other side. Repeat with remaining mixture.

Serves 4.

- ■ Recipe best made close to serving.
- ■ Freeze: Not suitable.
- ■ Microwave: Not suitable.

◎ Add 3 rashers finely chopped, cooked bacon to corncake batter.

LEFT: From left: Paprika Crumbed Pumpkin with Ricotta Topping, Saucy Vegetables with Parsley Thyme Dumplings.
ABOVE: Ratatouille with Corncakes.

Left: Jug and ceramics from Powder Blue; glass from Accoutrement; tiles from Country Floors.

STIR-FRIED SESAME CABBAGE AND ZUCCHINI

2 green shallots
3 medium zucchini
¼ cup (60ml) vegetable oil
¼ small red cabbage, shredded
1 clove garlic, crushed
1 tablespoon sesame oil
¼ cup (35g) sesame seeds, toasted
2 tablespoons honey
2 teaspoons sweet chilli sauce
¼ cup (60ml) light soy sauce

Cut shallots into 3cm lengths. Cut zucchini in half lengthways, then into 3cm lengths. Heat 2 tablespoons of the vegetable oil in wok or pan, add shallots, zucchini, cabbage and garlic, stir-fry until cabbage is just wilted. Transfer mixture to bowl, add remaining oils, and remaining ingredients; mix well. Serve hot or cold.

Serves 4.

- Recipe can be made 3 hours ahead.
- Storage: Covered, in refrigerator.
- Freeze: Not suitable.
- Microwave: Not suitable.

NUTTY BUBBLE AND SQUEAK WITH HERB TOMATOES

2 medium potatoes, chopped
250g pumpkin, peeled, chopped
1 medium onion, finely chopped
1 medium carrot, finely chopped
½ cup (60g) frozen peas
1 cup (80g) shredded cabbage
1 tablespoon chopped fresh parsley
¼ cup (60ml) olive oil
½ cup (60g) chopped
**   roasted hazelnuts**
1 tablespoon stale wholemeal
**   breadcrumbs**
½ cup (60g) grated tasty cheese

HERB TOMATOES
250g cherry tomatoes, halved
2 tablespoons olive oil
2 cloves garlic, crushed
1 tablespoon shredded fresh basil
2 teaspoons chopped fresh oregano
2 teaspoons chopped fresh thyme

Boil, steam or microwave potatoes until tender, drain, mash well; cool. Boil, steam or microwave remaining vegetables until tender; drain, rinse under cold water, drain well; cool. Combine all vegetables and parsley in bowl; mix well.

Heat oil in large frying pan, spread vegetable mixture evenly into pan, cook, without stirring, until browned underneath. Remove from heat, sprinkle with combined nuts, breadcrumbs and cheese, grill until top is lightly browned. Stand 5 minutes, cut into wedges, serve with warm herb tomatoes.

Herb Tomatoes: Combine tomatoes, oil, garlic and herbs in baking dish, bake, uncovered, in moderate oven about 10 minutes or until tomatoes are heated through.

Serves 4.

- Recipe best made just before serving.
- Freeze: Not suitable.
- Microwave: Vegetables suitable.

⊙ Omit pumpkin; replace with 150g chopped silverside in vegetable mixture.

VEGETABLE KEBABS WITH CORIANDER COCONUT CREAM

2 large zucchini
1 small red pepper
1 small yellow pepper
1 small green pepper
12 baby potatoes
300g cauliflower, chopped
1 tablespoon vegetable oil

CORIANDER COCONUT CREAM
1 tablespoon vegetable oil
4 green shallots, chopped
2 cloves garlic, crushed
1 teaspoon grated fresh ginger
2 teaspoons ground cumin
1 teaspoon paprika
1½ cups (375ml) coconut cream
1 tablespoon lime juice
2 tablespoons mild chilli sauce
1½ tablespoons chopped
**   fresh coriander**

Cut each zucchini into 6 pieces. Cut each pepper into 12 large pieces.

Boil, steam or microwave zucchini, peppers, potatoes and cauliflower separately until just tender; drain. Thread vegetables onto 12 skewers, brush with oil, grill or barbecue until browned and hot. Serve with coriander coconut cream.

Coriander Coconut Cream: Heat oil in pan, add shallots, garlic, ginger, cumin and paprika, cook, stirring, until shallots are soft. Add cream, juice, sauce and coriander, simmer, uncovered, 3 minutes.

Makes 12.

- Recipe can be prepared a day ahead.
- Storage: Covered, separately, in refrigerator.
- Freeze: Not suitable.
- Microwave: Vegetables suitable.

⊙ Thread 24 scallops onto skewers with vegetables.

RIGHT: Clockwise from left: Stir-Fried Sesame Cabbage and Zucchini, Nutty Bubble and Squeak with Herb Tomatoes, Vegetable Kebabs with Coriander Coconut Cream.

Plates and jug from Accoutrement; fabric from Les Olivades.

GARLIC ROAST PEPPERS WITH OLIVE CROUTES

1 medium red Spanish onion
½ cup (125ml) olive oil
2 medium red peppers, quartered
2 medium green peppers, quartered
2 medium yellow peppers, quartered
10 unpeeled cloves garlic
⅓ cup (50g) pine nuts, toasted
150g goats' cheese

TOMATO SALSA
1 medium red Spanish onion
425g can tomatoes
½ teaspoon sugar
⅓ cup (80ml) water

OLIVE CROUTES
1 large French bread stick
½ cup (125ml) olive oil
1 tablespoon olive paste

Cut onion into 8 wedges. Combine onion, oil, peppers and garlic in large baking dish. Bake, uncovered, in moderate oven 1 hour. Add salsa and nuts, bake 30 minutes, turning vegetables occasionally. Serve vegetables with crumbled cheese.
Tomato Salsa: Cut onion into 8 wedges. Combine onion, undrained crushed tomatoes and remaining ingredients in pan, simmer, uncovered, until thickened.
Olive Croutes: Cut bread into 1.5cm slices. Place bread on oven tray, brush with combined oil and paste, toast in moderately hot oven about 10 minutes.
Serves 4.

- ■ Recipe can be prepared a day ahead.
- ■ Storage: Vegetables, covered, in refrigerator. Croutes, airtight container.
- ■ Freeze: Not suitable.
- ■ Microwave: Tomato salsa suitable.

- ◉ Add 8 slices salami to baking dish with salsa and nuts.

MUSHROOM, GINGER AND TOFU STIR-FRY

375g packet tofu, drained
1 tablespoon vegetable oil
1 clove garlic, crushed
2 teaspoons chopped fresh ginger
100g oyster mushrooms, halved
200g button mushrooms, halved
200g Swiss brown
**   mushrooms, halved**
1 medium red pepper, thinly sliced
⅓ cup (80ml) vegetable stock
1 tablespoon light soy sauce
1 tablespoon honey
1 teaspoon sesame oil
½ teaspoon sambal oelek
2 teaspoons cornflour
3 green shallots, chopped

Cut tofu into 2cm cubes. Heat vegetable oil in pan, add tofu, garlic and ginger, cook, stirring, until tofu is lightly browned. Add mushrooms, cook, stirring, until lightly browned. Add pepper and blended stock, sauce, honey, sesame oil, sambal oelek and cornflour, stir over heat until sauce boils and thickens, stir in shallots.
Serves 4.

- ■ Recipe best made just before serving.
- ■ Freeze: Not suitable.
- ■ Microwave: Not suitable.

LAYERED ITALIAN-STYLE SALAD WITH CREAMY EGGS

6 hard-boiled eggs, chopped
2 tablespoons sour cream
2 tablespoons mayonnaise
2 green shallots, chopped
1 large red pepper
100g sugar snap peas
30g butter
125g button mushrooms, quartered
2 cloves garlic, crushed
6 lettuce leaves, shredded
⅓ cup (80g) drained sun-dried
**   tomatoes, sliced**
¼ cup shredded fresh basil
⅔ cup (80g) pitted black
**   olives, quartered**
50g snow pea sprouts
¼ cup (20g) parmesan cheese flakes
⅓ cup (80ml) French dressing

Combine eggs, sour cream and mayonnaise in bowl; mash until smooth, stir in shallots. Quarter pepper, remove seeds and membrane. Grill pepper, skin side up, until skin blisters and blackens. Peel away skin, cut pepper into thin strips. Boil, steam or microwave sugar snap peas until just tender; drain, rinse under cold water, drain.

Heat butter in pan, add mushrooms and garlic, cook, stirring, until mushrooms are browned; drain on absorbent paper, cool.

Just before serving, divide lettuce between 4 plates, top with egg mixture, tomatoes, basil, olives, pepper strips,

ugar snap peas, mushroom mixture, sprouts and cheese; drizzle with dressing. Serves 4.

■ Recipe can be prepared several hours ahead.
■ Storage: Covered, in refrigerator.
■ Freeze: Not suitable.
■ Microwave: Sugar snap peas suitable.

LEFT: From back: Mushroom, Ginger and Tofu Stir-Fry, Garlic Roast Peppers with Olive Croutes.

ABOVE: From left: Spring Salad with Tarragon Butter Croutes, Layered Italian-Style Salad with Creamy Eggs.

Above: Plates from Powder Blue; fabric from Redelman & Son Pty Ltd.

SPRING SALAD WITH TARRAGON BUTTER CROUTES

We used edible, unsprayed flower petals such as nasturtium, marigold and borage in this recipe.

1 bunch (about 250g) fresh thin asparagus, halved
1 medium avocado, sliced
8 drained artichoke hearts, halved
125g mixed salad leaves
12 hard-boiled quail eggs, halved
¼ cup (35g) chopped macadamias, toasted
2 tablespoons edible flower petals

TARRAGON BUTTER CROUTES
6 slices white bread
40g soft butter
1 tablespoon chopped fresh tarragon

DRESSING
1½ tablespoons red wine vinegar
2 tablespoons hazelnut oil
¼ cup (60ml) extra virgin olive oil
2 teaspoons grated lemon rind
1 tablespoon chopped fresh chervil

Boil, steam or microwave asparagus until just tender; drain, rinse under cold water, drain. Divide asparagus, avocado, artichokes, salad leaves and eggs between 4 plates. Top with nuts and tarragon butter croutes, drizzle with dressing, sprinkle with petals.
Tarragon Butter Croutes: Remove crusts from bread, cut each slice into 8 triangles. Combine butter and tarragon in bowl; mix well. Spread butter mixture over croutes, place on oven tray, toast in moderate oven about 20 minutes.
Dressing: Combine all ingredients in jar; shake well.

Serves 4.

■ Croutes and dressing can be made a day ahead.
■ Storage: Croutes, airtight container. Dressing, covered, in refrigerator.
■ Freeze: Not suitable.
■ Microwave: Asparagus suitable.

◉ Replace quail eggs with 500g cooked scallops.

GINGER VEGETABLE STIR-FRY

425g can young corn spears, drained
1 tablespoon vegetable oil
1 teaspoon sesame oil
2 cloves garlic, crushed
1 tablespoon grated fresh ginger
1 tablespoon sweet chilli sauce
1 medium red pepper, sliced
1 medium green pepper, sliced
1 medium yellow pepper, sliced
1 bunch (about 250g) fresh asparagus
125g snow peas
4 green shallots, sliced
⅔ cup (160ml) water
¼ cup (60ml) light soy sauce
2 teaspoons cornflour

Cut corn spears in half lengthways. Heat oils in wok or pan, add garlic, ginger and chilli sauce, stir over heat until fragrant. Add peppers, asparagus, snow peas and shallots, stir-fry until vegetables are just tender. Add corn and blended water, sauce and cornflour, stir over heat until mixture boils and thickens.

Serves 4.

■ Recipe best made just before serving.
■ Freeze: Not suitable.
■ Microwave: Not suitable.

◉ Stir-fry 400g thinly sliced rump steak in batches before stir-frying vegetables. Combine with vegetable mixture just before serving

EGGPLANTS WITH TOMATO SAUCE AND PESTO

2 medium eggplants
plain flour
oil for deep-frying
¼ cup (40g) pine nuts, toasted
1 cup (50g) firmly packed
    watercress sprigs

TOMATO SAUCE
1 tablespoon olive oil
1 medium onion, sliced
2 cloves garlic, crushed
2 x 410g cans tomatoes
½ teaspoon sugar

PESTO
1½ cups fresh basil leaves
⅓ cup (25g) grated parmesan cheese
1 clove garlic, crushed
⅓ cup (50g) pine nuts
¼ cup (60ml) olive oil

Cut eggplants into 1cm slices, toss in flour, shake away excess flour. Deep-fry eggplant in batches in hot oil until browned; drain on absorbent paper. Serve eggplant with tomato sauce, pesto, nuts and watercress.

Tomato Sauce: Heat oil in pan, add onion and garlic, cook, stirring, until onion is soft. Add undrained crushed tomatoes and sugar, simmer, uncovered, stirring occasionally, until thickened.

Pesto: Blend or process basil, cheese, garlic and nuts until smooth, add oil gradually in thin stream while motor is operating.

Serves 4 to 6.

■ Tomato sauce and pesto can be made a day ahead.
■ Storage: Covered, separately, in refrigerator.
■ Freeze: Not suitable.
■ Microwave: Not suitable.

◉ Serve 4 grilled quail, halved, with eggplant.

BAKED KUMARA IN LEMON CREAM SAUCE

600g kumara
1 tablespoon olive oil
1 medium onion, finely chopped
1 clove garlic, crushed
2 teaspoons grated lemon rind
1 small red pepper, chopped
½ cup (40g) grated parmesan cheese
¼ cup (35g) chopped pistachios
1 tablespoon chopped
    pistachios, extra
½ teaspoon seasoned pepper

LEMON CREAM SAUCE
300ml thickened cream
¼ cup (60ml) lemon juice

Cut kumara into 5mm slices. Boil, steam or microwave kumara until tender; drain.

Heat oil in pan, add onion and garlic, cook, stirring, until onion is soft. Transfer mixture to bowl, stir in rind, pepper, cheese and nuts. Layer kumara and onion mixture in ovenproof dish (1.5 litre/ 6 cup capacity), pour over lemon cream sauce, sprinkle with extra nuts and pepper. Bake, uncovered, in moderate oven about 30 minutes, or until mixture is heated through.

Lemon Cream Sauce: Combine cream and juice in pan, simmer, uncovered, about 5 minutes or until reduced by half.

Serves 4.

■ Onion mixture and lemon sauce can be made a day ahead.
■ Storage: Covered, separately, in refrigerator.
■ Freeze: Not suitable.
■ Microwave: Kumara suitable.

HERB TOFU BALLS IN TOMATO SAUCE

2 tablespoons vegetable oil
1 small onion, finely chopped
375g tofu, drained
½ cup (35g) stale wholemeal
    breadcrumbs
2 tablespoons plain flour
2 tablespoons chopped fresh parsley
2 teaspoons light soy sauce
¼ teaspoon garlic powder
1 tablespoon chopped fresh chives
2 tablespoons shredded fresh basil

TOMATO SAUCE
1 tablespoon vegetable oil
1 medium onion, finely sliced
½ cup (125ml) dry red wine
810g can tomatoes

Heat 1 tablespoon of the oil in pan, add onion, cook, stirring, until soft. Process tofu with half the onion mixture until smooth. Transfer mixture to bowl, stir in remaining onion mixture, crumbs, flour, parsley, sauce, garlic and chives. Roll level tablespoons of mixture into balls, place in baking dish, brush with remaining oil. Bake in moderately hot oven about 40

minutes or until browned, turning once. Serve with tomato sauce and basil.

Tomato Sauce: Heat oil in pan, add onion, cook, stirring, until soft. Add wine, undrained crushed tomatoes, simmer, uncovered, until mixture is slightly thickened.

Serves 4.

■ Recipe best made close to serving.
■ Freeze: Not suitable.
■ Microwave: Tomato sauce suitable.

◉ Add ⅔ cup (100g) chopped, cooked chicken or ham to sauce.

LEFT: From back: Eggplants with Tomato Sauce and Pesto, Ginger Vegetable Stir-Fry. ABOVE: From back: Herb Tofu Balls in Tomato Sauce, Baked Kumara in Lemon Cream Sauce.

Left: Cutlery from Accoutrement; tiles from Country Floors. Above: Plate, jug and basket from Accoutrement; fabric from I. Redelman & Son Pty Ltd.

CURRIED EGGS IN PAPPADUM NESTS

4 spiced pappadums
oil for deep-frying
2 teaspoons vegetable oil
1 tablespoon curry powder
1 teaspoon ground cumin
1 teaspoon ground coriander
½ teaspoon garam masala
4 green shallots, chopped
½ cup (125ml) sour cream
½ cup (125ml) mayonnaise
8 hard-boiled eggs, quartered
1 medium green pepper, chopped
2 tablespoons chopped
fresh coriander

CHILLI VEGETABLES
1 medium carrot
2 medium zucchini
1 medium red pepper
1 tablespoon sweet chilli sauce
1 tablespoon vegetable oil
½ teaspoon sesame oil

Dip pappadums into hot water until soft; pat dry on absorbent paper.

Mould 1 pappadum into oiled metal ladle.

Place second oiled ladle on top of pappadum; press together. Deep-fry pappadum nest in hot oil, using ladles to mould shape until firm; carefully remove pappadum from ladle with spatula; drain on absorbent paper. Repeat with remaining pappadums.

Heat vegetable oil in pan, add spices and shallots, cook, stirring, until shallots are soft. Combine shallot mixture, sour cream, mayonnaise, eggs, pepper and coriander in bowl; mix well. Spoon egg mixture into pappadum nests, serve with chilli vegetables.

Chilli Vegetables: Cut carrot, zucchini and pepper into thin strips. Add carrot to pan of boiling water for 10 seconds; drain, rinse under cold water, drain. Combine carrot with remaining ingredients in bowl; mix well.

Serves 4.

- Pappadum nests can be made several days ahead.
- Storage: Airtight container.
- Freeze: Not suitable.
- Microwave: Carrot suitable.

◉ Add 250g sliced, cooked chicken to chilli vegetables.

BARBECUED VEGETABLES WITH PARSNIP PUREE

400g kumara
2 medium chokoes
3 medium carrots
6 medium potatoes
1 large eggplant, sliced
8 spring onions, halved
¼ cup (60ml) olive oil
¼ cup chopped fresh thyme
½ teaspoon celery salt

PARSNIP PUREE
3 cups (750ml) vegetable stock
750g parsnips, chopped
⅓ cup (80ml) olive oil
¼ cup (60ml) cream

Cut kumara, chokoes, carrots and potatoes into wedges, boil, steam or microwave separately until just tender; drain. Brush all vegetables with oil, barbecue or grill until lightly browned and hot. Sprinkle with combined thyme and salt, serve with parsnip puree.

Parsnip Puree: Bring stock to boil in pan, add parsnips, simmer, covered, about 15 minutes or until very soft; drain. Blend or process parsnips with remaining ingredients until smooth.

Serves 6.

- Parsnip puree can be made a day ahead.
- Storage: Covered, in refrigerator.
- Freeze: Not suitable.
- Microwave: Vegetables and puree suitable.

LEFT: From left: Barbecued Vegetables with Parsnip Puree, Curried Eggs in Pappadum Nests.

China from Home and Garden on the Mall; wire basket and serviette from Barbara's Storehouse.

MUSHROOMS IN POLENTA BEER BATTER WITH EGGPLANT

1 medium eggplant
coarse cooking salt
¼ cup (60ml) olive oil
8 (about 360g) cup mushrooms
oil for deep-frying

POLENTA BEER BATTER
⅔ cup (100g) self-raising flour
¼ cup (35g) polenta
½ cup (125ml) beer

DRESSING
⅓ cup (80ml) extra virgin olive oil
1 tablespoon balsamic vinegar
¼ teaspoon sugar
2 small fresh red chillies,
    finely chopped
1 tablespoon shredded fresh basil

Cut eggplant into 1cm slices (you need 8 slices for this recipe). Sprinkle eggplant with salt, stand 20 minutes. Rinse under cold water; drain, pat dry with absorbent paper. Brush eggplant slices with olive oil, grill on both sides until browned.

Dip mushrooms in batter, deep-fry in hot oil until lightly browned; drain on absorbent paper. Serve eggplant topped with mushrooms and dressing.

Polenta Beer Batter: Combine flour and polenta in bowl, gradually stir in beer, stir until combined.

Dressing: Combine all ingredients in jar; shake well.

Serves 2.

- ■ Recipe best made just before serving.
- ■ Freeze: Not suitable.
- ■ Microwave: Not suitable.

HONEY SOY KEBABS WITH FRUITY PILAF

1 medium red pepper
1 medium zucchini
375g tofu, drained
1 medium onion
12 button mushrooms
12 cherry tomatoes

MARINADE
2 tablespoons honey
2 tablespoons light soy sauce
2 cloves garlic, crushed
1 teaspoon sesame oil

FRUITY PILAF
½ cup (75g) sliced dried apricots
½ cup (80g) sultanas
40g butter
1½ cups (300g) long-grain rice
3 cups (750ml) vegetable stock
½ cup (80g) pine nuts, toasted
2 tablespoons chopped fresh chives

Cut pepper into 2cm pieces and zucchini into 1cm slices. Cut tofu into 24 cubes and onion into 12 wedges. Thread all ingredients onto 12 skewers, place in shallow dish, pour over marinade, cover, refrigerate, several hours or overnight.

Drain kebabs, reserve marinade. Grill or barbecue kebabs, brushing occasionally with reserved marinade, until browned and cooked through. Serve with fruity pilaf.

Marinade: Combine all ingredients in bowl; mix well.

Fruity Pilaf: Place apricots and sultanas in heatproof bowl, cover with boiling water, stand 15 minutes; drain.

Heat butter in pan, add rice, stir until grains are coated with butter. Add stock, simmer, uncovered, 5 minutes, cover, simmer over low heat further 10 minutes. Remove from heat, stand, covered, 5 minutes. Add fruit, nuts and chives to rice mixture; mix well.

Serves 4 to 6.

- ■ Kebabs best prepared a day ahead.
- ■ Storage: Covered, in refrigerator.
- ■ Freeze: Not suitable.
- ■ Microwave: Not suitable.

- ◉ Replace tofu with 250g cubed, cooked lamb.

SPICY CORN AND TOMATOES WITH CRISP OKRA

2 tablespoons vegetable oil
2 large onions, sliced
1 clove garlic, crushed
½ teaspoon dried chilli flakes
2 x 440g can corn kernels, drained
390g can pimientos,
**   drained, chopped**
425g can tomatoes
½ cup (125ml) cream
1 teaspoon sugar
2 tablespoons chopped
**   fresh coriander**

CRISP OKRA
250g okra
½ cup (75g) plain flour
1 egg
2 tablespoons milk
2½ cups (375g) cornmeal
oil for deep-frying

Heat oil in pan, add onions, garlic and chilli, cook, stirring, until onions are soft. Stir in corn, pimientos, undrained crushed tomatoes and cream, simmer, uncovered, until slightly thickened. Stir in sugar and coriander. Serve topped with crisp okra.

Crisp Okra: Rinse okra, cut in half lengthways. Toss okra in flour, dip into egg and milk, toss in cornmeal. Deep-fry okra in batches in hot oil until lightly browned; drain on absorbent paper.

Serves 4.

■ Crisp okra best cooked just before serving.
■ Freeze: Not suitable.
■ Microwave: Corn mixture suitable.

◉ Add 4 cooked, sliced pork sausages to corn mixture.

LEFT: Mushrooms in Polenta Beer Batter with Eggplant.
BELOW: From left: Spicy Corn and Tomatoes with Crisp Okra, Honey Soy Kebabs with Fruity Pilaf.

Left: Fork from Accoutrement; tiles from Country Floors. Below: Basket and place mat from Accoutrement.

ASIAN-STYLE SALAD WITH LIME CHILLI DRESSING

200g green beans
1 bunch (about 250g) fresh asparagus
500g broccoli, chopped
1 medium red pepper, sliced
1 medium yellow pepper, sliced
4 green shallots, sliced
2 tablespoons chopped
    fresh coriander
2 tablespoons chopped fresh mint
50g snow pea sprouts

LIME CHILLI DRESSING
½ cup (125ml) water
1 teaspoon grated lime rind
⅓ cup (80ml) lime juice
1 tablespoon light soy sauce
1 tablespoon sweet chilli sauce

Cut beans and asparagus into 4cm lengths. Boil, steam or microwave beans, asparagus and broccoli until just tender; drain, rinse under cold water, drain.

Combine beans, asparagus and broccoli with remaining ingredients in bowl, add dressing; mix well.

Lime Chilli Dressing: Combine all ingredients in pan, simmer, uncovered, for 2 minutes; cool.

Serves 4.

- ■ Recipe best made just before serving.
- ■ Freeze: Not suitable.
- ■ Microwave: Suitable.

- ◉ Add 4 cooked, sliced lamb fillets to salad.

TWICE-BAKED CELERIAC SOUFFLES WITH SPINACH

60g butter
1 small onion, finely chopped
1 teaspoon white mustard seeds
300g celeriac, grated
¼ cup (35g) plain flour
1 cup (250ml) milk
2 tablespoons grated tasty cheese
3 eggs, separated
2 tablespoons chopped fresh chives
2 cloves garlic, crushed
1 bunch (about 650g) English
    spinach, shredded

CHIVE HOLLANDAISE
2 egg yolks
1½ tablespoons tarragon vinegar
250g butter, melted
2 tablespoons chopped fresh chives

Grease 8 ovenproof moulds (½ cup/125ml capacity). Heat half the butter in pan, add onion and seeds, cook, stirring, until onion is soft. Add celeriac, cook, stirring, until soft, stir in flour. Remove from heat, gradually stir in milk, stir over heat until mixture boils and thickens; stir in cheese. Transfer mixture to bowl, cool slightly; stir in egg yolks and chives.

Beat egg whites in small bowl until soft peaks form, fold into mixture. Spoon into prepared moulds, place in baking dish, pour in boiling water to come halfway up sides of moulds. Bake in moderate oven about 30 minutes or until firm, remove from dish, stand until warm.

Turn souffles onto greased oven tray, top with chive hollandaise. Bake in moderately hot oven about 10 minutes or until browned. Heat remaining butter in pan, add garlic and spinach, cook until spinach is wilted. Serve souffles with spinach.

Chive Hollandaise: Combine yolks and vinegar in heatproof bowl, whisk over simmering water until thickened slightly. Remove from heat, whisk in hot butter in thin stream (do not mix in residue). Stir in chives.

Makes 8.

■ Recipe best made just before serving.
■ Freeze: Not suitable.
■ Microwave: Not suitable.

◎ Add 2 chopped, cooked bacon rashers to souffle mixture.

VEGETABLE PARCELS WITH SPICED CREAM

8 baby new potatoes
1 medium carrot, sliced
½ bunch (about 125g) fresh asparagus
75g oyster mushrooms
120g sugar snap peas
2 medium zucchini, sliced
125g cherry tomatoes, halved
½ cup loosely packed fresh basil leaves
1 tablespoon grated fresh ginger
2 green shallots, sliced
2 cloves garlic, crushed
60g butter
2 teaspoons grated lime rind
⅓ cup (80ml) lime juice

SPICED CREAM
1 cup (250ml) sour cream
1 teaspoon sambal oelek
2 tablespoons chopped fresh coriander
½ teaspoon garam masala

Boil, steam or microwave potatoes, carrot and asparagus separately until just tender; drain.

Cut 4 large pieces of foil. Divide potatoes, carrot, asparagus, mushrooms, peas, zucchini, tomatoes and basil between foil pieces. Combine ginger, shallots, garlic, butter and rind in bowl; mix well. Top vegetables with butter mixture, drizzle with juice. Fold up edges to form a parcel, seal firmly. Place parcels on oven tray, bake in moderately hot oven 30 minutes or until vegetables are cooked. Serve topped with spiced cream.

Spiced Cream: Combine all ingredients in bowl; mix well.

Serves 4.

■ Can be prepared 3 hours ahead.
■ Storage: Covered, in refrigerator.
■ Freeze: Not suitable.
■ Microwave: Potatoes, carrot and asparagus suitable.

◎ Omit potatoes. Add 500g uncooked seafood to vegetables before wrapping.

LEFT: From left: Twice-Baked Celeriac Souffles with Spinach, Asian-Style Salad with Lime Chilli Dressing.
BELOW: Vegetable Parcels with Spiced Cream.

Left: China from Waterford Wedgwood.

WHOLEMEAL ZUCCHINI AND NUT SLICE

1½ cups (240g) blanched almonds
1 tablespoon vegetable oil
1 clove garlic, crushed
1 medium onion, chopped
4 eggs, lightly beaten
¼ cup (60ml) milk
1 cup (70g) stale wholemeal
    breadcrumbs
3 medium zucchini, grated
1 medium carrot, grated
1 cup (125g) grated tasty cheese

Grease 15cm x 25cm loaf pan, line with foil, grease foil. Process nuts until finely chopped. Heat oil in pan, add garlic and onion, cook until onion is soft; cool. Combine all ingredients in bowl; mix well. Spoon mixture into prepared pan, bake, uncovered, in moderate oven about 1 hour or until firm. Remove from pan; serve sliced.
Serves 4.

■ Recipe can be made a day ahead.
■ Storage: Covered, in refrigerator.
■ Freeze: Not suitable.
■ Microwave: Not suitable.

◎ Add 4 slices chopped mortadella to slice with remaining ingredients.

VEGETABLE SALAD WITH CHILLI PEANUT DRESSING

300g new potatoes, halved
250g cauliflower, chopped
250g green beans, sliced
2 medium carrots, sliced
½ small red cabbage, shredded
2 cups (160g) bean sprouts
1 long green cucumber, chopped
4 hard-boiled eggs, quartered

PEANUT DRESSING
30g butter
1 medium onion, finely chopped
1½ teaspoons curry powder
1 teaspoon ground cumin
1 teaspoon plain flour
2 teaspoons sweet chilli sauce
½ cup (175g) crunchy peanut butter
1 tablespoon brown sugar
400ml coconut cream

Boil, steam or microwave potatoes, cauliflower, beans and carrots separately until just tender; drain, rinse under cold water, drain.

Place cabbage on plate, top with cooked vegetables, sprouts, cucumber and eggs; drizzle with peanut dressing.
Peanut Dressing: Heat butter in pan, add onion, cook, stirring, until soft. Add curry powder, cumin, flour and chilli sauce, cook, stirring, 2 minutes. Stir in peanut butter, sugar and coconut cream. Simmer, uncovered, about 10 minutes or until slightly thickened.

Serves 4.

■ Peanut sauce can be made 2 days ahead.
■ Storage: Covered, in refrigerator.
■ Freeze: Not suitable.
■ Microwave: Vegetables suitable.

◎ Add 350g sliced, cooked chicken to vegetable salad.

GREEN VEGETABLE CASSEROLE

2 tablespoons vegetable oil
1 medium onion, chopped
500g baby new potatoes, quartered
1 stick celery, chopped
1 medium green pepper, chopped
2 medium zucchini, chopped
200g green beans, chopped
3 cups (750ml) vegetable stock
1 cup (125g) frozen green peas
1 bunch (about 250g) fresh
    asparagus, chopped
4 green shallots, chopped
½ cup chopped fresh parsley
¼ cup shredded fresh basil
1 tablespoon chopped fresh oregano
1 teaspoon seasoned pepper
4 poached eggs
⅓ cup (25g) grated parmesan cheese
2 tablespoons pine nuts, toasted

Heat oil in pan, add onion and potatoes, cook, stirring, until onion is soft. Stir in celery, pepper, zucchini, beans and stock, simmer, uncovered, about 15 minutes or until vegetables are tender. Stir in peas and asparagus, simmer, uncovered, until tender. Stir in shallots, herbs and pepper. Spoon vegetable mixture into 4 serving bowls, top with poached eggs; sprinkle with cheese and nuts.

Serves 4.

■ Recipe best made just before serving.
■ Freeze: Not suitable.
■ Microwave: Suitable.

POTATO ROSTI WITH GOLDEN SHALLOT COMPOTE

4 large (about 800g) old potatoes, coarsely grated
1 teaspoon seasoned pepper
½ cup (125ml) olive oil
125g mixed salad leaves
½ cup (50g) chopped walnuts

GOLDEN SHALLOT COMPOTE
2 medium red peppers
40g butter
500g golden shallots, peeled
¼ cup (60ml) dry white wine
2 tablespoons sugar
¼ cup (60ml) sherry vinegar
2 tablespoons chopped fresh thyme

DRESSING
2 tablespoons walnut oil
1 tablespoon extra virgin olive oil
1½ tablespoons sherry vinegar

Combine potatoes and pepper in bowl; mix well. Heat half the oil in pan, add ¼ cup (60ml) of potato mixture, flatten with spatula. Cook until browned and crisp underneath, turn, cook other side. Repeat with remaining mixture using remaining oil when necessary. Drizzle salad leaves with dressing, sprinkle with nuts. Serve with potato rosti and golden shallot compote.
Golden Shallot Compote: Quarter peppers, remove seeds and membranes. Grill peppers, skin side up, until skin blisters and blackens. Peel away skin, slice peppers. Heat butter in pan, add

shallots, cook, covered, 10 minutes, add wine, sugar and vinegar, simmer, uncovered, about 20 minutes, or until shallots are tender. Stir in peppers and thyme, stir until heated through.
Dressing: Combine all ingredients in jar; shake well.

Serves 4.

■ Golden shallot compote and dressing can be prepared a day ahead.
■ Storage: Covered, separately, in refrigerator.
■ Freeze: Not suitable.
■ Microwave: Not suitable.

◉ Add 100g sliced pastrami to salad leaves.

LEFT: From front: Vegetable Salad with Chilli Peanut Dressing, Wholemeal Zucchini and Nut Slice.
ABOVE: From left: Green Vegetable Casserole, Potato Rosti with Golden Shallot Compote.

119

FRESH HERB SAUCE AND FOCCACIA WITH VEGETABLES

12 baby carrots
12 baby beetroot
8 baby new potatoes
2 bunches (500g) fresh asparagus
1 witlof
8 radishes

FRESH HERB SAUCE
½ cup firmly packed fresh
    basil leaves
½ cup firmly packed flat-leafed
    parsley
2 tablespoons chopped
    fresh tarragon
¼ cup chopped fresh dill
2 green shallots, chopped
2 cloves garlic, crushed
2 tablespoons drained capers
¼ cup (20g) grated romano cheese
1 cup (250ml) extra virgin olive oil

FOCCACIA
3 teaspoons (10g) dried yeast
1 teaspoon sugar
1 cup (250ml) warm water
¼ cup (60ml) olive oil
3 cups (450g) plain flour
1 teaspoon salt
⅓ cup fresh rosemary leaves
1 teaspoon rock salt
cracked black pepper

Boil, steam or microwave carrots, beetroot, potatoes, and asparagus separately until just tender. Serve warm with witlof leaves and radishes. Serve with fresh herb sauce and foccacia.

Fresh Herb Sauce: Process herbs, shallots, garlic, capers and cheese with quarter of the oil until smooth. Add remaining oil gradually while motor is operating.

Foccacia: Combine yeast, sugar and water in bowl, cover, stand in warm place about 10 minutes or until frothy; stir in oil. Sift flour and salt into bowl, stir in yeast mixture. If necessary, add a little extra warm water to give a soft dough. Knead dough on floured surface about 10 minutes or until smooth. Place dough in oiled bowl, cover, stand in warm place about 1 hour or until doubled in size.

Turn dough onto floured surface, knead until smooth. Press dough into greased 20cm x 30cm lamington pan, cover, stand in warm place about 40 minutes or until doubled in size. Prick dough with fork, brush with a little extra oil, sprinkle with rosemary, rock salt and pepper. Bake in hot oven about 25 minutes or until browned.

Serves 4 to 6.

- Fresh herb sauce can be made a day ahead.
- Storage: Covered, in refrigerator.
- Freeze: Foccacia suitable.
- Microwave: Vegetables suitable.

◉ Cook 500g beef fillet on barbecue or griddle pan until tender. Serve sliced thinly with vegetable platter.

MEXICAN-STYLE CORN AND PEPPER SALAD

4 fresh corn cobs
1 cos lettuce
2 medium tomatoes, chopped
1 medium red Spanish onion,
    thinly sliced
2 medium red peppers, sliced
2 medium green peppers, sliced
1 medium avocado, chopped
200g packet corn chips

DRESSING
½ cup (125ml) olive oil
¼ cup (60ml) lime juice
2 tablespoons chopped
    fresh coriander
2 tablespoons sweet chilli sauce

Boil, steam or microwave corn until tender; drain. Barbecue or grill corn until lightly browned all over, slice thickly. Combine corn, torn lettuce and remaining ingredients in bowl; drizzle with dressing.

Dressing: Combine all ingredients in jar; shake well.

Serves 4.

- Recipe best made close to serving.
- Freeze: Not suitable.
- Microwave: Corn suitable.

◉ Add 250g cooked, sliced chorizo sausage to salad.

MUSHROOM AND FETA CHEESE LASAGNE WITH FRESH DILL

375g packet tofu, drained
1 clove garlic, crushed
1 tablespoon red wine vinegar
2 teaspoons honey
1 tablespoon light soy sauce
30g butter
1 medium onion, chopped
250g flat mushrooms, chopped
1 tablespoon lemon juice
1 tablespoon chopped fresh dill
1 medium zucchini, chopped
2 tablespoons plain flour
½ bunch (about 325g) English spinach, shredded
1 teaspoon sugar
1½ cups (375ml) tomato puree
40g feta cheese

CHEESE SAUCE
30g butter
3 teaspoons plain flour
¾ cup (180ml) milk
50g feta cheese

Wrap tofu in absorbent paper, squeeze out excess liquid. Cut tofu horizontally into 5mm slices. Combine tofu, garlic, vinegar, honey and sauce in shallow dish, cover, refrigerate overnight.

Drain tofu; reserve marinade. Heat butter in pan, add onion and mushrooms, cook, stirring, until onion is soft. Add juice, dill and zucchini, cook, stirring, until zucchini is soft. Add flour, stir until combined. Stir in spinach, sugar, puree and reserved marinade, stir over heat until mixture boils and thickens.

Cover base of 4 ovenproof dishes (1 cup/250ml capacity) with half the tofu, top with half the mushroom mixture, remaining tofu, then remaining mushroom mixture. Spoon over cheese sauce, sprinkle with crumbled cheese.

Place dishes on oven tray, bake in hot oven about 15 minutes or until browned.
Cheese Sauce: Melt butter in pan, add flour, stir over heat until mixture bubbles. Remove from heat, gradually stir in milk, stir over heat until sauce boils and thickens; stir in crumbled cheese.

Serves 4.
- ■ Tofu best prepared a day ahead.
- ■ Storage: Covered, in refrigerator.
- ■ Freeze: Not suitable.
- ■ Microwave: Cheese sauce suitable.

◉ Sprinkle 2 finely chopped bacon rashers over lasagne instead of cheese.

LEFT: Fresh Herb Sauce and Foccacia with Vegetables.
BELOW: From left: Mushroom and Feta Cheese Lasagne with Fresh Dill, Mexican-Style Corn and Pepper Salad.

Left: Tiles from Country Floors. Below: Tray from Accoutrement; fabric from Les Olivades.

Glossary

Here are some terms, names and alternatives to help everyone use and understand our recipes perfectly.

AGAR-AGAR: seaweed in shreds or powder; sets at room temperature. We used powdered agar-agar.

ALCOHOL: is optional, but gives a particular flavour. Use fruit juice or water instead.

ALMONDS:

Blanched: nuts with skin removed.

Flaked: sliced nuts.

Slivered: nuts cut lengthways.

BACON RASHERS: bacon slices.

BEETROOT: regular round beet.

BLACK BEAN SAUCE: made from fermented whole and crushed soya beans, water and wheat flour.

BOK CHOY: Chinese chard.

BREADCRUMBS:

Packaged: use fine packaged breadcrumbs.

Stale: 1- or 2-day-old bread crumbed by grating, blending or processing.

BUCKWHEAT: seeds are roasted and used whole or made into flour; cracked wheat can be substituted.

BURGHUL: cracked wheat.

BUTTER: use salted or unsalted (also called sweet) butter; 125g is equal to 1 stick butter.

BUTTERMILK: is now made by adding a culture to skim milk to give a slightly acid flavour; skim milk can be substituted.

CELERIAC: tuberous root with a celery-like flavour.

CHICK PEAS: garbanzos.

CHINESE BROCCOLI: gai lum.

CHOKO: chayote or christophenes.

CINNAMON STICK: dried inner bark of the shoots of the cinnamon tree.

COCONUT: desiccated coconut.

Cream: available in cans and cartons.

Flaked: flaked coconut flesh.

Milk: available in cans.

Shredded: strips of dried coconut.

CORIANDER: also known as cilantro and Chinese parsley; is available fresh, ground and in seed form.

CORNFLOUR: cornstarch.

CORNMEAL: ground corn (maize); similar to polenta but pale yellow and finer. One can be substituted for the other, but results will vary.

COUSCOUS: a fine cereal made from semolina.

CREAM: light pouring cream, also known as half and half.

Light sour: a less dense, commercially cultured soured cream; do not substitute this for sour cream.

Sour: a thick, commercially cultured soured cream.

EGGPLANT: aubergine.

FENNEL: has a slight aniseed taste when fresh, ground or in seed form.

Bulb: is eaten cooked or uncooked.

FILLO PASTRY: also known as phyllo dough; comes in tissue-thin pastry sheets bought chilled or frozen.

FIVE SPICE POWDER: a pungent mixture of ground spices which include cinnamon, cloves, fennel, star anise and Szechwan peppers.

FLOUR:

Besan: flour from ground chick peas.

Buckwheat: flour from buckwheat.

Chick pea: flour from ground chick peas; also known as gram or besan flour.

Plain: unbleached all-purpose flour.

Self-raising: substitute plain (all-purpose) flour and baking powder in the proportions of 1 cup (150g) plain flour to 2 level teaspoons baking powder. Sift together several times before using.

Wholemeal plain: wholewheat flour without the addition of baking powder.

Wholemeal self-raising: wholewheat self-raising flour; add baking powder as for plain self-raising to make wholemeal self-raising flour.

GARAM MASALA: a combination of cardamom, cinnamon, cloves, coriander, cumin and nutmeg in varying proportions.

GHEE: a pure butter fat available in cans.

GHERKIN: cornichon.

GINGER: fresh, green or root ginger.

GOW GEES PASTRY: wonton wrappers, spring roll or egg pastry sheets can be substituted.

GRAINS: see picture on page 123.

HOI SIN SAUCE: a thick, sweet Chinese barbecue sauce made from salted black beans, onion and garlic.

HUMMUS: a paste of chick peas, tahini, garlic, lemon juice and olive oil.

JALAPENO PEPPERS: imported, canned, pickled hot chillies.

JERUSALEM ARTICHOKE: root vegetable.

JUNIPER BERRIES: dried berries of an evergreen tree.

KAFFIR LIME LEAVES: citrus or lime leaves; are bought in dried form.

KONBU: kelp seaweed.

KUMARA: orange sweet potato.

LAMINGTON PAN: 20cm x 30cm rectangular pan, 3cm deep.

LEMON GRASS: available from Asian food stores and needs to be bruised or chopped before using.

LENTILS: dried pulses. There are many varieties, usually identified and named after their colour; see page123.

MAPLE-FLAVOURED SYRUP: golden/pancake syrup; honey can be substituted.

MIRIN: sweet rice wine.

MIXED SPICE: a blend of ground spices usually consisting of cinnamon, allspice and nutmeg.

MUSHROOMS: are sold in 3 stages of growth; button, cup and flat.

Button: are small, white and tightly closed with a mild flavour. Ideal for salads, sauces, pickles, garnishes.

Cup: have a full-bodied flavour and firm texture. Ideal for soups, pies and casseroles.

Flat: are fully mature with a rich, unique flavour.

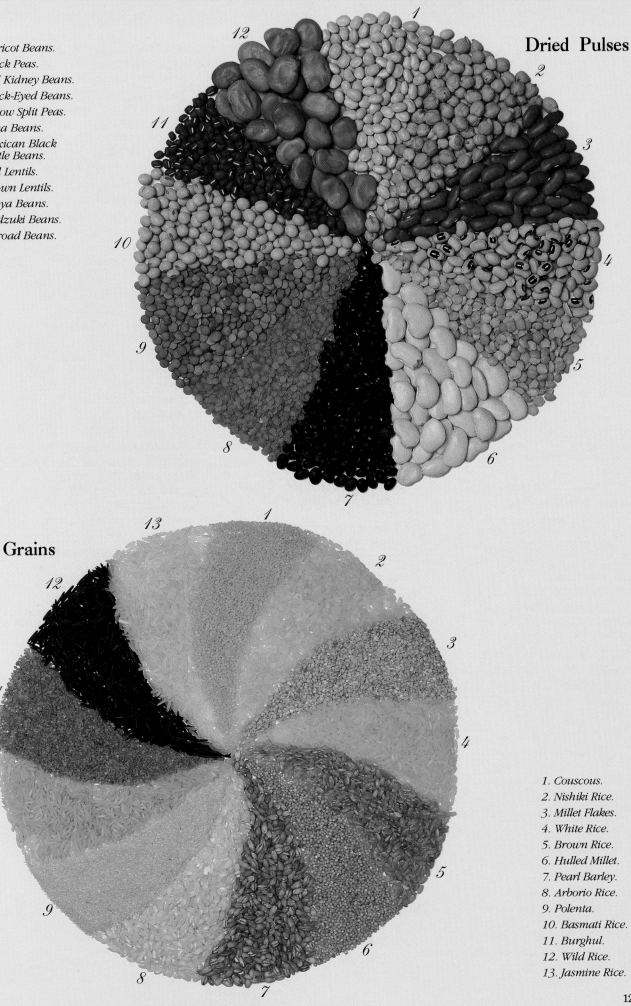

Dried Pulses

1. Haricot Beans.
2. Chick Peas.
3. Red Kidney Beans.
4. Black-Eyed Beans.
5. Yellow Split Peas.
6. Lima Beans.
7. Mexican Black
   Turtle Beans.
8. Red Lentils.
9. Brown Lentils.
10. Soya Beans.
11. Adzuki Beans.
12. Broad Beans.

Grains

1. Couscous.
2. Nishiki Rice.
3. Millet Flakes.
4. White Rice.
5. Brown Rice.
6. Hulled Millet.
7. Pearl Barley.
8. Arborio Rice.
9. Polenta.
10. Basmati Rice.
11. Burghul.
12. Wild Rice.
13. Jasmine Rice.

123

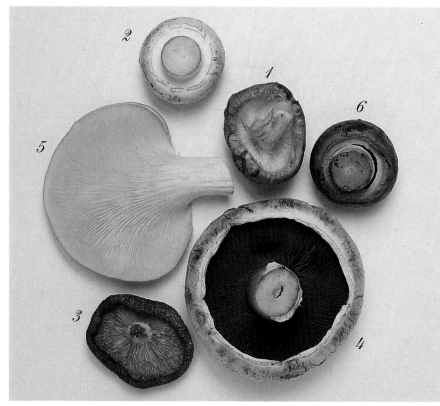

1. Shitake Mushrooms. 2. Button Mushrooms. 3. Chinese Dried Mushrooms.
4. Flat Mushrooms. 5. Oyster Mushrooms. 6. Swiss Brown Mushrooms.

NORI: a type of dried seaweed.

OKRA: immature seed pod, also called lady's fingers.

OLIVE PASTE: is made from olives, olive oil, salt, vinegar and herbs.

PANCETTA: cured pork belly; bacon can be substituted.

PARSLEY, FLAT-LEAFED: also known as Continental parsley or Italian parsley.

PASTRAMI: seasoned smoked beef.

PEPITAS: dried pumpkin seeds.

PEPPERS: capsicums or bell peppers.

PICKLED PINK GINGER: vinegared ginger in paper-thin shavings.

POLENTA: see Cornmeal.

PRAWNS: shrimp.

PROSCIUTTO: uncooked, unsmoked ham, cured in salt.

PULSES: see picture on page 123.

REFRIED BEANS: available in cans.

RICE VERMICELLI: rice noodles.

RIND: zest.

SAFFRON: available in strands or ground form. The quality varies greatly.

SAKE: rice wine.

SAMBAL OELEK (also ulek or olek): a paste made from ground chillies and salt.

SEASONED PEPPER: bottled combination of black pepper, sugar and bell peppers.

SESAME OIL: made from roasted, crushed white sesame seeds. Do not use for frying.

SESAME SEEDS: can be black or white; we used white.

SHALLOTS:

Golden: very small brown onions with strong flavour.

Green: also known as scallions or green onions.

SNOW PEAS: mange tout.

SORREL: has broad, oval leaves with a bitter, slightly sour taste.

SOY SAUCE: made from fermented soya beans.

SPECK: Smoked pork.

SPINACH:

Silverbeet: use green, leafy parts.

English: a soft-leaved vegetable, more delicate in taste than silverbeet.

SPRING ROLL PASTRY SHEETS: see Gow Gees Pastry.

STOCK POWDER: 1 cup (250ml) stock is the equivalent of 1 cup (250ml) water plus 1 crumbled stock cube (or 1 teaspoon stock powder). If preferred, see Make Your Own Stock, right.

SUGAR: coarse, granulated table sugar, also known as crystal sugar.

SUGAR SNAP PEAS: small pods with small peas; eat whole, cooked or uncooked.

SULTANAS: seedless white raisins.

SUNFLOWER SEED KERNELS: from dried sunflower seeds.

TABASCO SAUCE: made with vinegar, hot red peppers and salt. Use in drops.

TAHINI PASTE: made from crushed sesame seeds.

TERIYAKI SAUCE: based on Japanese soy sauce; contains sugar, spices and vinegar.

TOFU: made from boiled, crushed soya beans. We used firm tofu.

TOMATO:

Cherry tomatoes: Tom Thumb tomatoes, small and round.

Paste: concentrated puree.

Sauce: tomato ketchup.

Sun-dried: dried tomatoes, sometimes bottled in oil.

Teardrop: small, yellow tomatoes.

TORTILLAS: flat bread considered the national bread of Mexico; available in supermarkets.

VINE LEAVES: available in brine in jars and packets.

WASABI PASTE: green horseradish.

WATER CHESTNUTS: small, white, crisp bulbs with a brown skin. We used canned water chestnuts.

WHEATGERM: small, creamy flakes milled from the embryo of the wheat.

WITLOF: chicory or Belgian endive.

WORCESTERSHIRE SAUCE: spicy sauce.

YEAST: allow 2 teaspoons (7g) dried yeast to each 15g compressed yeast if substituting one for the other.

ZUCCHINI: courgette.

MAKE YOUR OWN STOCK

VEGETABLE STOCK

1 large carrot, chopped
1 large parsnip, chopped
2 onions, chopped
6 sticks celery, chopped
4 bay leaves
2 teaspoons black peppercorns
3 litres (12 cups) water

Combine all ingredients in large pan, simmer, uncovered, for 1½ hours; strain.

Makes about 5 cups.

■ Stock can be made 4 days ahead.
■ Storage: Covered, in refrigerator.
■ Freeze: Suitable.
■ Microwave: Not suitable.

Index

QUICK CONVERSION GUIDE

Wherever you live in the world you can use our recipes with the help of our easy-to-follow conversions for all your cooking needs. These conversions are approximate only. The difference between the exact and approximate conversions of liquid and dry measures amounts to only a teaspoon or two, and will not make any difference to your cooking results.

MEASURING EQUIPMENT

The difference between measuring cups internationally is minimal within 2 or 3 teaspoons' difference. (For the record, 1 Australian metric measuring cup will hold approximately 250ml.) The most accurate way of measuring dry ingredients is to weigh them. When measuring liquids use a clear glass or plastic jug with metric markings.

If you would like the measuring cups and spoons as used in our Test Kitchen, turn to page 128 for details and order coupon. In this book we use metric measuring cups and spoons approved by Standards Australia.

● a graduated set of four cups for measuring dry ingredients; the sizes are marked on the cups.
● a graduated set of four spoons for measuring dry and liquid ingredients; the amounts are marked on the spoons.
● 1 TEASPOON: 5ml.
● 1 TABLESPOON: 20ml.

NOTE: NZ, CANADA, USA AND UK ALL USE 15ml TABLESPOONS.
ALL CUP AND SPOON MEASUREMENTS ARE LEVEL.

DRY MEASURES

METRIC	IMPERIAL
15g	½oz
30g	1oz
60g	2oz
90g	3oz
125g	4oz (¼lb)
155g	5oz
185g	6oz
220g	7oz
250g	8oz (½lb)
280g	9oz
315g	10oz
345g	11oz
375g	12oz (¾lb)
410g	13oz
440g	14oz
470g	15oz
500g	16oz (1lb)
750g	24oz (1½lb)
1kg	32oz (2lb)

LIQUID MEASURES

METRIC	IMPERIAL
30ml	1 fluid oz
60ml	2 fluid oz
100ml	3 fluid oz
125ml	4 fluid oz
150ml	5 fluid oz (¼ pint/1 gill)
190ml	6 fluid oz
250ml	8 fluid oz
300ml	10 fluid oz (½ pint)
500ml	16 fluid oz
600ml	20 fluid oz (1 pint)
1000ml (1 litre)	1¾ pints

WE USE LARGE EGGS WITH AN AVERAGE WEIGHT OF 60g

HELPFUL MEASURES

METRIC	IMPERIAL
3mm	⅛in
6mm	¼in
1cm	½in
2cm	¾in
2.5cm	1in
5cm	2in
6cm	2½in
8cm	3in
10cm	4in
13cm	5in
15cm	6in
18cm	7in
20cm	8in
23cm	9in
25cm	10in
28cm	11in
30cm	12in (1ft)

HOW TO MEASURE

When using the graduated metric measuring cups, it is important to shake the dry ingredients loosely into the required cup. Do not tap the cup on the bench, or pack the ingredients into the cup unless otherwise directed. Level top of cup with knife. When using graduated metric measuring spoons, level top of spoon with knife. When measuring liquids in the jug, place jug on flat surface, check for accuracy at eye level.

OVEN TEMPERATURES

These oven temperatures are only a guide; we've given you the lower degree of heat. Always check the manufacturer's manual.

	C° (Celsius)	F° (Fahrenheit)	Gas Mark
Very slow	120	250	1
Slow	150	300	2
Moderately slow	160	325	3
Moderate	180	350	4
Moderately hot	190	375	5
Hot	200	400	6
Very hot	230	450	7

TWO GREAT OFFERS FROM THE AWW HOME LIBRARY

Here's the perfect way to keep your Home Library books in order, clean and within easy reach. More than a dozen books fit into this smart silver grey vinyl folder. PRICE: Australia $9.95; elsewhere $19.95; prices include postage and handling. To order your holder, see the details below.

All recipes in the AWW Home Library are created using Australia's unique system of metric cups and spoons. While it is relatively easy for overseas readers to make any minor conversions required, it is easier still to own this durable set of Australian cups and spoons (photographed). PRICE : Australia: $5.95; New Zealand: $A8.00; elsewhere: $9.95; prices include postage & handling.
This offer is available in all countries.

TO ORDER YOUR METRIC MEASURING SET OR BOOK HOLDER:

PHONE: Have your credit card details ready. **Sydney:** (02) 260 0035; **elsewhere in Australia:** 008 252 515 (free call, Mon-Fri, 9am-5pm) or *FAX* your order to (02) 267 4363 or *MAIL* your order by photocopying or cutting out and completing the coupon below.

PAYMENT: **Australian residents:** We accept the credit cards listed, money orders and cheques. **Overseas residents:** We accept the credit cards listed, drafts in $A drawn on an Australian bank, also English, New Zealand and U.S. cheques in the currency of the country of issue.
Credit card charges are at the exchange rate current at the time of payment.

Please photocopy and complete coupon and fax or send to:
AWW Home Library Reader Offer, ACP Direct, PO Box 7036, Sydney 2001.

❏ Metric Measuring Set ❏ Holder
Please indicate number(s) required.

Mr/Mrs/Ms _____

Address _____

_____

Postcode_____ Country _____
Ph: ( ) _____ Bus. Hour:_____
I enclose my cheque/money order for $ _____ payable to ACP Direct

OR: please charge my:

❏ Bankcard ❏ Visa ❏ MasterCard ❏ Diners Club ❏ Amex

☐☐☐☐☐☐☐☐☐☐☐☐☐☐☐☐ Exp. Date ___/__

Cardholder's signature_____

(Please allow up to 30 days for delivery within Australia. Allow up to 6 weeks for overseas deliveries.)
Both offers expire 31/12/93.   AWRB92